D1508496

DREAM

COACHING

DREAM
COACHING

ACHIEVE THE LIFE YOU WERE
MEANT TO LEAD BY UNDERSTANDING

YOUR DREAMS

DAVID C. LOHFF

Author of
THE DREAM DIRECTORY & DREAMS

RUNNING PRESS
PHILADELPHIA · LONDON

9 8 7 6 5 4 3 2 1
Digit on the right indicates the number of this printing

Library of Congress Control Number 2003111201
ISBN 0-7624-1693-9

Cover photo by Weaver Lilly
Cover design by Whitney Cook
Interior design by Eric Horner
Project manager and rewrite editor: Deborah Grandinetti
Development editing by Sally Clark Sheola, in consultation with Alice Feinstein
Copyediting by Jane Sherman
Typography: Garamond, Futura

This book may be ordered by mail from the publisher.
Please include $2.50 for postage and handling.
But try your bookstore first!

Running Press Book Publishers
125 South Twenty-second Street
Philadelphia, Pennsylvania 19103-4399

Visit us on the web!
www.runningpress.com

To my children, who go to bed every night
expecting sweet dreams

CONTENTS

Acknowledgments

I am deeply indebted to my editor, Deborah Grandinetti, who endured my formative thinking about this book. With optimism and insight that a fresh perspective lay beneath my ramblings, she guided me to craft this work. Her encouragement significantly clarified my vision. Anyone else would have given up before the finish line.

I am indebted as well to two of the great thinkers of our era, Dr. Henry Cloud and Dr. John Townsend, who have written great works on the soul and its growth. If I have offered any fresh vision, it is because I have stood on the shoulders of giants. Their work on the spirituality of growth and relationship has been a constant inspiration to me.

Further, I thank the many people who generously shared their stories so that you can study them. The dreams of real people in the real world form the bulk of this work. Because of their sharing, this book can be practical and immediate rather than theoretical and obscure. In every case, the dreamers *dreamed* their lives would be better tomorrow than they were today. The Divine answered their desire with cues for guidance, growth, and hope.

Finally, I thank my wife and all those who tolerated my grouchiness and inaccessibility as the work took on its final form. Writing a book happens in the midst of everyday living, and inspiration is sometimes a laborious affair.

We have forgotten the age-old fact that God speaks chiefly through dreams and visions.

—Carl Jung

INTRODUCTION

The Dream That Started Me on My Journey

Two decades ago, when I was an awkward adolescent struggling for a sense of competence as an athlete, I had an amazing experience. The night before I was to play soccer for the local township, I dreamed of myself on the playing field. The details were unusually vivid and lifelike. I knew exactly where I was positioned on the field. I saw my teammate pass the ball to me, and each and every challenge I overcame as I ferried the ball across the field and shot it successfully past the opposing team's goal line.

The dream itself wasn't remarkable.

What *was* remarkable was what happened the next day. I was in the same exact position on the field as I had been in my dream, when I saw the same teammate pass the ball to me in *exactly* the same way as he had in my dream. And I, just as I had in my dream, received the pass and moved the soccer ball across the field, past the very same obstacles, and scored. Every single detail I had dreamed ten hours earlier was accurate. Somehow, I had seen the whole thing unfold in my dreams ten hours before it happened. But how? By what power was I able to see the future in such vivid and precise detail?

I was completely enthralled by the experience—and fascinated by the potential of dreams. That was the day I started looking "within," rather than outside myself, for the power to succeed in my life. That experience impressed upon me the power of a dream to interact with—and perhaps even *change*—waking reality. I was so taken by what happened that I could never again look at life in exactly the same way. The incident launched me on a lifelong journey to better understand this inner power to "know" truth without the benefit of information available to the five senses.

Since that very special dream, I have found myself returning again and again to dreams for guidance. Through timely warnings, encouragement, and inspiration, my dreams have helped me become a better husband, father, employee, and a better person overall. They have illuminated the steps I must take to develop into that joyous and fulfilled person the Creator intended for me to become.

The same has been true for the clients I have counseled as a Baptist pastor, counselor, and spiritual guide. They, too, have found that dreams are invaluable for discovering the inner promptings of the soul—and regaining the sense of direction necessary to maintain balance in a world that excels at throwing people off balance. They have learned, as I have, that there is much to be gained by listening to the inner guidance of the soul.

When you learn to correctly interpret *your* dreams, the soul guidance they contain will light the way for you to create more happiness in your life, too.

A Classic Problem-Solving Dream

While my soccer dream foreshadowed the success to come, dreams can also provide the inspiration that stimulates success. Some dreams bring *aha!* moments, inspired answers to challenges at home or at work.

Here's a classic example of a work-related problem-solving dream, drawn from the life of Elias Howe, the Massachusetts man who invented the sewing machine. Back in Howe's day, all clothes were hand-sewn with a needle and thread. The distinguishing characteristic of a hand-sewing needle, still true in this day, is that the "eye"—the opening for thread—is at the top of the needle. The bottom of the needle is pointed, to help pierce the fabric.

In 1835, Howe apprenticed to a machinist at a local textile mill. Over the next decade, he began thinking about how to automate sewing. But he was so locked in by the idea of a needle with an eye near the top that his initial efforts to create a successful machine failed. He put the eye in the center of the needle, but it kept breaking.

Then, at the age of 26, Howe had an amazing dream. As W.B. Kaempffert tells us in *A Popular History of American Invention,* vol. II (Scribner's 1924), Howe dreamed one night that he was captured by savages "who took him prisoner before their king." In that dream, Howe remembers the king saying: "I command you upon the pain of death to finish this machine at once."

The command caused the dreaming Howe to feel great fear. He knew the king meant business, surrounded as he was by warriors with sharp-pointed spears. Looking at the spears, Howe noticed that there were eye-shaped holes near the point. Voila! That was his answer. An "eye" close to the pointed end of the needle might solve the problem of needle breakage. After Howe realized this, he "sprang from his bed, and at once made a whittled model of the eye-pointed needle . . ." Sure enough, this kind of needle worked. And thus the sewing machine was born.

Other notables who have profited from dream inspiration include Niels Bohr, a physicist who "dreamed of a planetary system as a model for atoms as well as celestial bodies, and the composer Giuseppe Tartini, whose best-known work, *The Devil's Sonata,* was inspired by a dream.

The Problem-Solving Dream Taken to Diabolical Ends

An individual's ability to bring "dream intelligence" to bear on a problem doesn't always have a positive result. In a dark mind, the higher wisdom that flows from dreams can be twisted to terrifying ends. Such was the case with Osama bin Laden and his soccer dream publicized in a videotaped C.N.N. interview with him.

I got to thinking about bin Laden's dream because a Rhode Island newspaper reporter called me to ask about it. (I get these kinds of calls every once in a while, as the author of two previous dream books, *The Dream Directory* and *Dreams: More Than 350 Symbols and Interpretations.*)

The reporter saw the video and told me he was puzzled as to how bin Laden had connected the dots in his dream. In that video, bin Laden recounted a dream in which his al-Qaeda troops played soccer against Americans. In the dream, the soccer field changed into a scene with airplanes. That's what gave Osama bin Laden the idea to use airplanes in the horrifying 9/11 attacks.

The reporter asked me, "How did [Osama bin Laden] make the leap from soccer to airplanes?"

"It's a pretty logical progression," I told him. "The United States is a dominant 'player' on many fronts in the global community, but not in the game of soccer. Soccer is one of the great equalizers among countries. In this respect, soccer offered an opening for bin Laden, a way his little group could gain a competitive edge over the "infidels in the West."

I explained that soccer is a game that requires you to project the ball into your opponent's side of the field quickly, before the opponent can regroup and react to your attack. The surest way to succeed is to sail the ball through the air toward its target. Moving the ball on the ground may work, but sending it through the air is often the surest route to success.

At some point, I told the reporter, bin Laden must have asked himself how his group could quickly project its influence onto the Western "side of the field." It occurred to bin Laden that an airplane could serve the same purpose as the soccer ball. Of course, al-Qaeda, lacking an air force, would need to gain control of aircraft some other way. What is the most readily available supply of aircraft in the world? American commercial jets.

Can you see where this is going?

The dream provided bin Laden with an inkling of how he could "level the playing field," which was the toughest question. Then he used his logic to figure out how his people could best get hold of American commercial jets.

To the horror and dismay of many, bin Laden took the inspiration from his problem-solving dream and executed what was perhaps the most dastardly terrorist attacks this country has ever experienced. His dark mind, bent on revenge, used the "dream wisdom" destructively. Another man, having that dream, might well have decided to pit a top-notch soccer team from a Muslim country against one from the United States as a way to bring both cultures together on an even playing field. Sport has often been a means to build bridges in the global community. A soul-oriented interpretation of the dream would have included the possibility that the Americans and bin Laden could experience one another as "competitive equals" in the human story.

One could ask whether bin Laden's "inspiration" came from the same source that inspired my "prophetic" dream and Elias Howe's ingenious problem-solving solution. I would submit that each of these dreams came from a source of intelligence that is beyond everyday logic, but in not every case was the "dream wisdom" filtered through a positive, constructive mind. And that's what created the difference in the results.

In bin Laden's case, the fear that often drives fundamentalism—whether it's Islamic fundamentalism, or Christian, or Jewish, or any other form—found expression in anger and hatred. The force of that hatred took hold of bin Laden and caused him to interpret his dream in a way that would only create more pain and separation in the world, rather than harmony and wholeness, the agendas of the soul.

Certainly, America has not been the same since bin Laden executed his terrorist attack. The insecurity that attack has bred has created lingering anxiety throughout the nation. In times like these, when we are all looking for security in an uncertain world, "dream wisdom" becomes more important than ever. Dreams can steer us toward that which is good for us, and warn us away from that which will bring us harm. As simple as that seems, what could be more important? Just knowing what will be beneficial and what won't is half the battle of succeeding in life. Wouldn't you love to know in advance which relationships will bring fulfillment, and which will disappoint you? Or which career choices will make you happiest and most prosperous, and which will lead you to a dead end? Good dream interpretation skills can help you make the wisest choices in all aspects of your life.

PART I

Dreams Are the Voice of the Soul

CHAPTER 1

A Call to Soul Work

Out of a misty dream, our path emerges for a while,
then closes within a dream.

—Moss Hart

You carry within your soul an image of the person you are meant to be. Within that image is the "design" for a life that includes fulfilling personal relationships, a meaningful vocation, unique ways of using your gifts to serve the community, and other special knowledge that will make your life complete. In a sense, you could say that this is your "dream life," meaning the best possible life you could ever dream of having. It's almost as if you have already seen it, like a picture in a travel brochure that makes you think, "Yes, that is exactly where I want to be."

Chances are, if you are like most of us, there's a significant gap between your sense of how good things "could be" and how your life actually is. Maybe your personal life is fulfilling but you feel stymied in your career. Or vice versa. Or maybe both need a little—or a lot of—help.

Dreams can provide that help in a way that few other resources can. That's because they come from a special reservoir of intelligence inside of you—the soul, the animating principle in the body. (A body without a soul is little more than three dollars' worth of carbon compounds.) Let me define the soul for you and explain why "the soul" has reason to care whether or not you are fulfilled in your life. And then I will show you in practical terms how the soul uses dreams to help individuals who are leading less than satisfying lives to make the changes that lead to fulfilling lives.

The soul is that aspect of you that existed even before you were born and will continue to exist after your body dies. It is the immortal reflection of the Creative Force that has called you, and everything else, into being. As such it has the potential to develop and exercise all the powers associated with that Creative Force. In my spiritual tradition, the New Testament in the Bible explains the soul in this way: "Think ye not that ye are the Temple of God, and that the Spirit of God dwelleth within you?" That reflection of Spirit within each and every individual is the soul.

Think of dreams as one-way conversation coming from that all-powerful Creative Force through the soul into waking consciousness. Your choices and deepest questions turn that conversation into a dialogue.

If you are following along with me so far, it might occur to you to ask why the Creator is interested in having this kind of conversation with you. What does it matter to the Creator whether we are fulfilled or not? If we have fallen from the knowledge of our Divine origins, why should the Creator care?

It is because the Creator longs for us to return home, to that state of grace where there is no longer any separation. And it is the Creator's intention that we fulfill the Divine Purpose for which we were born, fully enjoying ourselves as we advance along the path of redemption. Finding the straightest path to fulfillment and redemption may require that we confront painful truths, summon up all of our courage, and make choices that, left to the devices of our personality, we might never willingly make. Yet, soul-inspired choices bring rich rewards.

Dreams Get to the Core of the Problem

This was certainly the case for one of my clients, who came to see me for counseling after a painful break-up. As we worked with her dreams, she began to explore the various influences in her life that shaped her relationships. At the root of the problem was her conviction that her own father, now deceased, had never really loved her. Together, we discovered that her feelings of unworthiness carried over into her adult relationships, causing her to choose men who were emotionally unavailable—just as her father was.

In the last stage of the dream work, my client—let's call her Vanessa—dreamed that her late father had come back to life to prove his love for her. The dream gave her the message that "there was no reason to mistrust that love." The dream gave her the opportunity to resolve the unhealed wounds in the father-daughter relationship and find peace within herself.

Up until that point, her feelings of unworthiness had not only played out in her love relationships, but in subtle ways, in all aspects of her life. At the deepest level, they also blocked her from receiving the abundant love the Creator intended her to experience through human relationships.

She later told me how much she appreciated dream work as a way to look beneath "the surface to uncover deeper, underlying issues I would not [otherwise] have paid attention to."

Finding Solace and Meaning in a Recurring Dream

Another client, a 36-year-old man who had suffered much trauma and abuse as a child, sent a recurring dream to the Web site I created to collect real-life dreams for this book. The man—let's call him "Victor"—later told me that as he read my reply, his entire body started to "buzz . . . at last things made sense . . . The childhood trauma I had been through, the protection I sought, the fears and strengths I had were all in there. Then I became amazed at how the dream was composed. How did I, as a young child unable to read, and lacking education, have images that were beyond my knowledge?"

In the dream, described in detail in Chapter 22, he is sometimes six years old and sometimes as old as age ten. He sees himself sitting on his twin bed, wearing blue pajamas. The bed is traveling on a very large escalator, but follows a straight line, instead of slanting down. Then, as he tells me,

One side of the escalator [my right] is a short wall I can't see over. The left wall is up to the ceiling. The space I am in is huge and dark except for the

light coming from the top of the escalator.

As I slowly travel down the escalator, my favorite cartoon characters appear on the left wall. They follow me during my ride. I can't hear them, so I try to figure out what they are saying to me, but they are cartoons, so I can't figure it out. I don't feel scared, but I know I'm doing something I am not supposed to do. At the end of the escalator is the large space. There is about 20 feet before the wall in front of me. The wall opposite the escalator is about 40 feet away. It is dark; the light from the top of the escalator has faded. There is some new light coming from the far wall.

As I turn to face the light, I see it's coming from what looks like a hallway that is located at the corner of the room, under the escalator. I am now very scared, and as I walk toward the hallway, I become more frightened. The floor is slanted down like a ramp. I never make it to the hallway/light.

Victor and I exchanged e-mails. He told me that "the dream is the same every time, but not so identical that I feel like I'm watching the same movie over and over. There are slight differences in the cartoon characters, their movements, and actions. I am always about the age of between six and ten. Same bedcovers and pajamas. In the beginning, I had this dream nightly, and by the time I was twenty-one, it was about once a year. Then three years passed before I had it again. Last night, eleven years later, I had it again, appearing about ten years old in the dream."

As I began to analyze it, it occurred to me that somehow it corresponded to life cycle changes that Victor had experienced. During childhood, each day can be a "new adventure." But ages twenty-one, twenty-four, and thirty-five can be milestones in the journey through young adulthood and toward middle adulthood.

The onset of the dream at age six was significant, as that is an age when a child is beginning to differentiate himself as an individual person, separate from his parents. For this to happen, both healthy connection and disconnection must be present.

Four significant elements were presented in the dream context: the bed, the escalator, the walls, and the light. Each of these had a mundane and unique feature. For example, the bed didn't slant on the escalator. It was the focal point because it moved Victor through the narrative.

The experiences were "not-scared," "seeing," "walking scared," and "not reaching the light." The fact that Victor experienced these feelings as he moved through the narrative was significant. He changed from "not scared" to "scared" in the same place, but changing places also caused a change in feelings.

"Not reaching" was an important experience because the implied goal of the dream was to find and experience the light. This was in spite of changing the mode of travel from riding to walking. It raised the question of whether Victor could conceive of reaching the goal at all.

After thinking about the dream, I sent an e-mail reply to Victor, asking him questions that would let us zero in on the relevance of this dream to his current life. Here is the thinking that informed my questions:

First, given the fact that he was the age of six at the onset of this dream, it seemed appropriate to ask him about his relationship to his parents. So I asked, "Has your mom been a pretty supportive parent in general? I'm not sure you've been readily able to connect with your dad."

The bed was the clue. There was ample comfort at the outset of the dream, reflecting motherly concern. However, there seemed to be an absence of independent ambition, as the child seemed dependent on moving via the bed.

My hunch proved correct.

"My mother has been very supportive and did a great job of raising kids while my father spent most of his time trying to manage his life from day to day," Victor told me. "I don't relate well to him at all and prefer not to have contact with him. We did have some contact, but it's minimal and basically consists of 'Hi, how are you? I'm fine. Good. Bye; take care.' At this point in my life, I don't expect more, and I'm not even sure I want more."

His answer spurred me to think about the importance of a child's relationship to his father. Feeling connected with Dad is a complex challenge for many 36-year-old adults, never mind a 6-year-old child. Even though Victor lacked the capacity to navigate these difficulties as a child, however, his soul was now hard at work on the father-attachment issue. Without that healthy connection to his father—and consequently, the inner part of him that reflected that relationship—he might move toward, but not necessarily reach, goals.

The continuation of the dream into adulthood raised another question, "How is this disconnection in childhood affecting your adult life?" I was very curious about how Victor perceived his life. Did he have a difficult time feeling that he was doing what he was meant to do?

"Yes," he told me. "I think that I have a purpose in life and have been unable to fulfill it because of some tragic events in childhood," he said.

The cartoon characters on the wall are noteworthy because they show how Victor comforted himself during these traumatic years. However, they were also troubling. They guided me toward a feeling that perhaps Victor was struggling to understand that what he experienced as a child was "really" happening to him.

"At a very young age some things happened to me that led to my shutting down, closing off, and hiding from the world," he said. "As a child, I didn't have the ability to understand what was occurring, so my only response was to shut down." (Remember that the cartoon characters were trying to say something that he didn't understand.)

Given the early onset of the dream, the initial impulse was to connect with Dad so Victor could experience himself as a loved son. But the connection was not made. As Victor has moved through life, the same feeling of unattained potential continues to construct the recurring dream narrative. Connection with others may at times be cut short due to the initial trauma he experienced by his lack of connection with his dad.

As an adult, Victor still carries in his soul the unrealized potential of achieving a greater sense of a meaningful and soul-sustaining connection if he can reach the light. "As an adult, I can deal with and overcome these elements," he said. "Now I believe that my gift is something to do with having a deeper understanding of some certain aspects of life, which I have not fully come to understand. But it is there, and I need to and will get it. At that time, I can share it with society. Until then I share it at a much lesser level with those I know."

Then he told me about his dream of writing a book "that will have a huge, positive effect, on a large number of people. Not some cult-type thing, but more to bring awareness to certain aspects of life and creating meaning and personal fulfillment for oneself," he said.

Notice how Victor perceives the resolution of his waking life. If he can connect this inner part of himself—the hurt, disconnected part—with a mass of people, he will heal others and himself in the process.

This dream was calling him toward healing and connection. It highlighted the importance of finding mentors to fill the voids in the personality created by his lack of connection to his father. At some level, Victor was able to do this successfully, as indicated by the fact that the dream had stopped for many years. Its reoccurrence was a sign that the soul was ready to pick this issue up again, and do even deeper work. In other words, as Victor begins to take steps toward creating the life of his dreams, he experiences the recurring dream again but makes progress toward resolving it.

Months later, Victor wrote to tell me that our work together helped him to find solace in his dream. "I have been able to use it to overcome the damage of my childhood experience. It has answered so many questions and generated so many more—such as how the brain and intelligence and dreams work.

"Having my dreams documented, I can allow it to rest," he said. "There may be times I look to it again to help me understand some small part of my life. Until then, I can continue to look at my new dreams and wonder what insight and advice they offer me."

Truth—the Growth-Stimulant

One of the most important resources to acquire in order to attain your personal growth goals is truth. Truth shows you clearly where you are in your life and the path you need to pursue to achieve your goals. Often it is hard for people to accept the truth of where they are in relationship to the life they were meant to live.

As these dreams indicate, the soul is ever calling us to greater health, well-being, and prosperity. In fact, the soul is biased towards these ends. It speaks through dreams to show you the gap, the truth between who you are right now and who you are intended to be. That's because the Creator wants each person to experience the very best out of life. The soul seeks to provide us with clear and healthy insight into our own unique gifts, skills, and talents; healthy and appropriate relationships with others, and a healthy connection to God.

Because this is the soul's aim, the solution it offers—whether through intuition, life circumstances, or dreams—typically differs from those the personality seeks. While the personality would prefer to manage the problem—in Cynthia's case, for instance, that might mean limiting her focus to her last relationship, instead of probing the deeper dynamics that have shaped all of her intimate relationships—the soul wants to get to the bottom of things. It wants to help you penetrate to the core of the problem and fully resolve it. And this is why it persistently confronts the dreamer with Truth, as in "the whole truth and nothing but the truth." Truth, in fact, is one of the greatest gifts that can come from a soul-inspired dream and an intelligent attempt to analyze it.

Truth is crucial to self-growth. Unless you can see yourself clearly, you can't see what is required to grow into the person you are intended to be. Without facing the truth, you'll never make progress. Have you ever known someone with a knack for staying stuck in painful situations? For people like that, life is one big crisis—one perpetuated by their inability to own up to reality and make the necessary changes to create the kind of life they want.

One of the greatest benefits of a dream is that the truth it reveals is not diluted by other's expectations of you. The "shoulds" and "should nots" that you carry around with you—jamming you up with other people's ideas of whom you *should* be—are absent in dreams. Most of us are "taught" to conform to other people's expectations of us, which makes it difficult, if not impossible to accept oneself, and the distinct reality that is "you," for better or worse.

But a good dream honestly represents where you are in relation to the person you are intended to be—even to the point of showing you the obstacles that you create for yourself. A good dream also shows you the truth about *you* regardless of how your parents, spouse, children, neighbors, and boss view you or treat you. In this way, it can bring you back to greater authenticity, a way of living in which you are true to yourself above all and living "from your soul." Sigmund Freud was indeed correct when he called dreams the "royal road to the soul."

At some level, I think most of us recognize this. That's probably why you bought this book, and why dreams hold so much fascination for many of us. It is also why people work hard to understand what their dreams mean. People who have heard that I am a "dream expert" will begin a conversation with me by saying, "I had the strangest dream last night . . . it was probably caused by [a troubling or powerful experience], and I think it means I should [change a behavior, seek a relationship, develop growth resources, avoid potential danger]." What they're telling me is that they realize the dreams must *mean something*.

I believe that they do. Not all dreams are significant, but the ones you carry into the day with you usually contain gems. And that's why, when someone tells me, "I had this dream . . ." I move to the edge of my seat, and prepare myself for a journey into the deep places of their soul.

CHAPTER 2

Distinguishing Personal Desires from Soul Wisdom

The dream is the small hidden door to the deepest and most intimate sanctum of the soul, which opens into that primeval cosmic night that was soul long before there was a conscious ego and will be soul far beyond what a conscious ego could ever reach.

—Carl Jung

When people call me a "dream expert," I humbly acknowledge the compliment. As both a cleric and a dream therapist, I have been listening to people seek growth, healing, comfort, and understanding for 15 years. In my listening, I've heard a voice repeat itself thousands of times from hundreds of people, desperate to be heard. It is the voice of aspiration, seeking understanding of today and resources to build a brighter tomorrow.

It often chooses to speak through dreams.

Yet my listening has also taught me that people often discard what they should heed and pay attention to what they should ignore. That leads many of us to chase after fantasies that can lead to ruin, while ignoring the guidance of the corrective, observing self that is present in many dream stories. This is ironic, given the fact that the dream's wisdom—emanating from the soul—is trying to reveal to us what we have to do to actualize a more fulfilling life. Sadly, we often jump to conclusions, based on our wants and desires, instead of making the effort to discern what the dream is *really* telling us. The bias in dream interpretation is always toward the dreamer's desires and prejudices.

Let me give you an example. The truth can be difficult to discern when you dream that that gorgeous guy or gal you've got your eye on has just asked you out. Your dream may be based more on your desire than that of the other person's, so a dream like this doesn't necessarily mean that a relationship with that attractive "other" is in the offing. Instead, it may be calling you to integrate into yourself the qualities that the "other" represents.

Soul Wisdom vs. Personality

Your soul understands who you really are and how to nurture your most authentic self, the person you are meant to become. That's not to say that the process of "becoming" is easy. Often, the desires of the personality conflict with those of the soul. What the soul understands about life, the personality often judges or condemns.

For instance, the soul understands that it is connected to the Divine, and therefore, to other souls. It also understands the needs human beings have for the essentials that sustain life and well-being, such as healthy food, clean water, and air, loving relationships (including those that provide emotional and sexual intimacy), a sense of belonging, a sense of purpose and meaning, etc. Our lives will not be satisfying until we can validate those needs for ourselves and meet them. Yet the personality often balks at opening itself to deep connected relationships with others, out of fear that it might experience rejection or pay another high price. It may also shrink away from natural and healthy desires, such as a desire for time alone to rejuvenate, or enough free time to express creativity, or the desire to express sexuality and experience intimate communion with another. In many cases, the obstacle is the personality's false belief that the individual doesn't deserve these pleasures, or alternately, that a "good person" is so selfless he or she shouldn't have any needs. Yet, when we dream, we plumb the depths, connecting with what is transcendent in life—those eternal truths that can restore wholeness.

Here's an example of a dream calling for wholeness. It came to urge the dreamer to honor her sexual nature, or else she would face unpleasant consequences. I will describe the dream first, then show you how we teased out the meaning so she could understand what the dream was telling her to do:

Dream Story: The Need to Reclaim Sexuality

A married, 24-year-old high school teacher told me the following dream:

I have had a sexual liaison with a student. I wake up literally shaking from the disgust I feel for my own actions.

DREAM COACHING

My intuition prompted me to ask her, "You don't really have a sexual outlet, do you?"

"No," she answered. "My spouse and I have been celibate and somewhat disconnected for quite a while,"

The dream was telling her to become proactive about attending to this facet of her life in appropriate ways rather than allowing starvation to continue. It was also a warning that there would be consequences if this marital situation continued as is. Maybe not the consequences she dreamed of, but real and painful ones nevertheless.

When we talked, the young teacher confessed that her imagination was running unchecked because she wasn't working on her marriage in waking life. But she was determined not to let herself act on the dream fantasy.

Determining Whether the Dream Is Expressing the Soul or the Personality

In this dream, the soul has the dominant voice. In these kinds of dreams, the dreamer wakes up feeling as though he or she must initiate some change, whether it's in a relationship, lifestyle, or behavior. The intended action will either help to materialize a coveted goal or avert an unwanted outcome.

In other dreams, the personality plays a more pronounced role. In fact, there's an entire category of dreams called "wish fulfillment" dreams in which the dream focuses his or her energies on achieving a preferred outcome without regard for the consequences to others.

But even when the soul is the dominant "voice" in a dream, it is up to the dreamer to receive its wisdom accurately. Many times, the wisdom is filtered through an imperfect understanding of what's essential in life and what leads to happiness. This tension can lead to dream images that conflict with one another, or are bizarre in some way.

In my experience, most dreams involve a conversation between the Creator, the soul, and the personality. Divine initiative, soul hunger, and personality expression weave a tapestry that, properly unraveled, reveal the elements of each in any given dream.

Why would the teacher seek to ignore her authentic needs for sexual expression? There could be many reasons. But the important thing to remember is this: the ways of the world fail to honor the deepest needs of human beings. Self-centered expectations warp relationships that should be pure, such as the mother-child or father-child relationships. And when the child experiences pain when reaching out to get her needs met, there is a good chance she will develop defenses in the hopes of protecting herself from ever getting hurt in that way again. Typically she—or he—may not be conscious of making this choice.

And just as typically, the needs of the soul are ignored as the personality seeks to preserve itself and stave off more pain. Often we prevent ourselves from having the best possible experience of *being* human, by choosing behaviors that arise out of a fear-based desire to survive without incurring further pain—no matter how much that choice oppresses our Spirit.

In fact, the personality develops in reaction to childhood pain and deprivation—being rejected or punished when you reach for what you want, or feeling the desperation and invalidation of the self that arises when your legitimate needs are completely ignored. Or maybe your caretakers imposed their adult needs upon the infant or immature you. Or maybe you misunderstood their behavior and made a judgment about your own worthiness in relation to their actions, as did the young woman who came to me for help in healing from the break-up of a relationship.

In these circumstances, children tend to develop defenses in an attempt to prevent themselves from experiencing more pain in the future. But here's the cost of that "protection:" As painful experiences accumulate, and with them, more defenses, you get further and further from the authentic self. Over time, you begin to confuse the "real self" with the personalities you have unconsciously created to cope with the imperfection you experienced in life.

Think of the personality as an "agent" you use to interact with the outside world. This agent lives on the periphery of your real life and develops strategies to meet its needs. Some personality types rely on seduction, others on helplessness, others on controlling or care-taking behaviors to manipulate others into meeting their needs. Others succumb to substance abuse or unhealthy compulsive behaviors to fill the void created when they reject essential aspects of the authentic self. Yet, underneath the personality is the unchanging soul, designed to exist in perfect harmony with its Creator and all of creation, and to express the unique purpose for which it was created.

Dreams can help you strip away the layers of the false self so you regain that wholeness you may not have experienced since early childhood. At night, when the demands of the day give way to the blessed silence of sleep, your soul has the freedom to speak honestly about your needs. Free, for a time, from the demands that your partners, parents, siblings, neighbors, bosses, or employees place upon you, you are free just to "be" you.

The Wisest Approach to Dream Interpretation

Because it can be tricky to separate the demands of your personality from the legitimate desires of your soul, as they may be expressed in a dream, you need a good system for analyzing your dreams. In my opinion, dream directories may be good starting points but, ultimately, they are not adequate for the job.

The folks who promote these directories tend to look at dreams as phenomena "outside" the person. When they do dream analysis, they look at the "meaning" of the dream symbols and conclude that the dream means the dreamer should do X, Y, or Z. Many traditional dream interpreters emphasize the personality at the expense of the soul, a choice akin to saying that the wrapping paper is the gift.

I prefer to look at dreams as guidance arising from the very life within you. Consequently, the 15 years I've spent listening to my clients as they work on their personal growth have moved me farther from traditional "dream work." "Soul work" seems to fit better. When I analyze dreams from this perspective, I put my focus not on the symbols but on what the person's inner self is trying to accomplish or reveal. And I converse with the person so I can understand how the actions in the dream relate to current circumstances in his or her life. I allow my intuition to inform my questions.

I will take you through this process over and over again in the dream stories that follow. The purpose is to teach you how to become your own dream coach, a skill that will serve you for the rest of your life.

CAN I INTERPRET MY OWN DREAMS?

If dream interpretation has been the sacred work of priests, shamans, medicine men, or the village elder, who are you to interpret your own dreams? Shouldn't this be left to the trained professionals?

Not on your life. If you don't attend to the sacred aspects of your being, who will? The fact is, you are the steward of your soul. A steward manages what has been entrusted to him. The Divine has entrusted your life to you.

Will you let the advertising, film, and broadcast industry influence how you live your life? Or do you want to live a life on your terms?

No doubt, people who live life as if it is a beer commercial do pretty well at it for a while. Just do your three score and ten (or more) and then you can push up daisies. The problem is that over time, if you are not connected to your life purpose, life sours. That's true, even if you've managed to acquire the best things money can buy, experienced the most intense physical pleasures, or delved deep into science or the arts, in the quest to make a name for yourself.

In the end, each of these pursuits can't guarantee the outcome we hunger for most—relationship or connection. Rich people get divorced, file for bankruptcy, and lose control of their lives. Famous people have messed-up children. People who crave intensity become bored with reality. People with great knowledge about inanimate objects lack the capacity to connect with other human beings. Even the highest level of success can't protect you from unsatisfying outcomes in life.

So you wake up one day feeling inexplicably sad or angry that this is all there is. You stop growing in your career because your capacity to function has reached its limit. Your spouse or partner moves out. Your kids start taking drugs because they feel isolated and can't comprehend the consequences of their actions. Anxiety, fear, or an addiction takes control of your life.

Sounds appealing, doesn't it?

A person without a dream is left at the mercy of the devouring forces of the world —especially those that threaten one's connection to the soul. Using your dreams to help you get "on purpose" is a much better choice By interpreting your dreams yourself, you get access to the finest coaching or life therapy your money can buy. That's because your dreams carry wisdom custom-made for you.

CHAPTER 3

Opening the "Gift" of the Dream

In a dream, the dreamer is simultaneously the author, designer, actor, prompter, stage manager, audience, and critic.

—Carl Jung

To effectively do the dream work in this book, you and your soul will need to become friends. One hallmark of true friends is that they accept each other as is. As your dream coach, I am asking you to consider opening yourself to the guidance in scary or troubling dreams, as well as those you consider "good" dreams. Regardless of how bizarre the content, try to think of each dream as gift waiting to be opened.

From my perspective, any dream that creates powerful feelings is a gift. A conflict that was resolved heroically, anxiety over a threat or seemingly illogical behavior, or feelings about an unresolved relationship that stayed with you from darkness into daylight, may evoke the powerful feelings.

This is a difficult truth to embarce at first. Most people hope for good dreams—in which their material desires are fulfilled—and they ignore so-called bad ones. Dreams are not good or bad based on how much fun you have in them. Ignoring a red light on while driving can be disastrous. Ignoring a dream just because it made you uncomfortable is equally foolish.

A dream gift can come in many forms. For instance:

- *A warning is a gift.* No matter how much you wanted to touch the stove as a child, your parents did you a favor by warning you not to, and denying you that experience.
- *A dream that prepares you for an upcoming challenge* is a gift.
- *A dream that signals independence,* even the discomfiting independence of being on your own, is a gift.
- *A dream that reveals your fear* is a gift when it helps you discern the risk-to-reward ratio of a particular experience.
- *Even a dream that in some way says "no," to an endeavor you were going to pursue or an ongoing behavior* can develop your character and help you avert disaster in your life and relationships.

Let's look at examples of these kind of dreams. One functioned as a warning, and another one told the dreamer "no."

Dream Story: Assurance Can Even Come from a Painful Dream

Kara came to see me after a particularly troubling dream. A strange juxtaposition of anguish and poise radiated from her, as tears fell from her blue eyes. For weeks, she had suspected that deceit was undermining the relationship she hoped would lead to marriage. Last night's dream, and a chance discovery the following morning, confirmed her worst fears:

> I was standing on a high cliff with him [her fiancé]. I told him I knew the truth [about his infidelity]. Then I turned and walked off the cliff. I fell for a long time but landed gently. After landing, I thought to myself, "It's amazing I'm not hurt." Then I started to walk alone, and I felt at peace as I walked.

As I listened, I knew that this was a powerful dream. Kara told me that after the dream, she turned on her fiancé's laptop computer, fished around, and soon found evidence that betrayed his infidelity. Yes, she felt hurt—but she was also being helped. A relationship carrying a crushing load of deceit was now exposed in the light of truth. And her dream told her that she would come out of this okay, and regain her peace. She couldn't see how everything would work, but she definitely sensed that her life, and perhaps even this relationship, could work.

By allowing the truth of the dream to inform her life, Kara realized that peace would come only once she took "the plunge"—and confronted her fiancé with what she knew. The dream truth freed her to choose what form her relationship would take.

DREAM COACHING

During the counseling session, Kara and I talked a lot about falling and continuing to walk. What would that be like? How did her dream represent that situation to her?

Her dream told her that the fall would be scary but it wouldn't harm her. In fact, the scariness of the fall would give way to a sense of peace that she hadn't experienced in the relationship in a long time. She knew she could face the truth and its consequences with confidence.

The dream called her to consider being together versus being apart. Through our discussion, she realized that being honest was more important to her than being afraid of whether this or any relationship was going to work out. If she were to follow the dream wisdom and "walk alone" for a time, rather than chasing after her fiancé, she would become more the person she wanted to be—someone who shares truth in a genuinely loving relationship but is no longer enslaved by deceit. The separation would also give her fiancé the opportunity to mature. She would let him know he'd have to choose between a relationship with her or his juvenile ways.

Although the morning started out badly, the dream helped her find the strength to better navigate these devastating circumstances in her life.

Why did Kara have the dream the night she had it, rather than a month earlier? I suspect that she wasn't ready beforehand. When she was ready, her soul spoke. Her relationship had been carrying the weight of deceit and its consequences—distance, lack of connection, and dishonesty—long enough. There was no path to healing other than confronting the truth.

While there are few things more frightening than confronting a truth that may end a relationship, the payoffs are tremendous. Kara affirmed her worth when she decided that she wouldn't settle for anything less than an open, honest, trusting love relationship that would lay a foundation for marriage.

Dreams can also help avert disaster in one's work life, as the dream narrative below suggests.

Dream Story: Thinking Twice About a Possible Career Change

Jerry, a man in his early thirties who was contemplating a career change to the military, reported dreaming:

> *I report for duty and have brought the wrong uniform. I am in blues, and everyone else is in khakis. No one salutes, even though I'm an officer. When I try to stow my belongings, I am housed in a gun turret. There's no phone, radio, nothing, just a hammock. I change to khakis to report for mealtime, and now everyone else is in whites. I begin speaking and realize I'm not speaking the correct language. I'm supposed to be speaking Hebrew, but I can't. Frustrated by the inability to speak, I wake up.*

DREAM COACHING

As I pondered the dream, I considered the fact that the absence of devices to contact the outside world was a troubling dream detail, since Jerry had a family. To be disconnected from them and also be unable to comprehend or connect with his military environment represented a difficult scenario. It seemed as though nothing would work as expected in that setting.

I decided to ask him, "You have authority issues, don't you?"

"Well, no, not really," he replied. "I despise most authority, but it's not an issue for me."

My thought was that the military didn't seem like a very promising career for someone with those attitudes. We explored the dream a little more. Could the military be a good home for someone with a heavy bent toward creativity and a "unique" personal style? The dreamer agreed that it probably couldn't.

After reflecting on the dream, the man withdrew his application for an officer's commission and sought a new career path. The dream may have averted potential disaster. Would it have come true? There's no way to tell. His desire to move his career forward was real. The motivation to get the growth resources to find his place in the world was legitimate. But the dream helped him see that a military career was not going to provide the resources he needed in a beneficial context.

Although each of these dreams made the dreamer uncomfortable, they forced Kara and Jerry to confront the truth about their circumstances and to make a crucial life-choice. The information was given to each of them so they might choose the course that would bring them the greatest fulfillment. The dream helped shift their perspective, opening new and better possibilities.

If you want to get the same results when you analyze your own dreams, these tips can help:

- When you awaken and respond to the dream gift, simply let it be what it is. Minimize the human tendency to elaborate on the dream by recalling the images and events without trying to draw immediate comparisons with your waking life. Recall the characters and events without including phrases such as "similar to my office" or "like the one I dated in school."

- "Secondary elaboration" occurs when you impose preconceived interpretations on your dreams to enforce what you want rather than what you need from life. For example, in recalling your dream, you may be exercising a certain amount of denial when you highlight the good parts ("I dreamed about a very attractive partner") and overlook the more difficult ones ("I found myself unable to respond"). This dream is speaking to the need to learn to experience connection with others.

- On the other hand, don't oversimplify the dreams you recall. A client once reported that her mother didn't come outside her house in the dream. I asked if she didn't come out because she was unwilling or because she was incapacitated. The answer to that query would significantly alter how I interpreted the dream. The details *are* important.

- As you record the dream, be honest, rather than obsessively detailed or editorially high-handed.
- Receive each dream with reverence and gratitude, regardless of how you perceive the substance of it.
- Realize that all the characters in your dreams—you and others—act within your perception of their potential. As Jung pointed out, the dreamer designs all the events of the dream.
- Recognize clues. In your dream, a mundane object may show up in an unfamiliar place. This is a clue that your soul is trying to represent a special gift in the dream, symbolized by the misplaced object.
- Recognize that often, there is much more inside than meets the eye. Dreams often have layer upon layer of meaning, representing several gifts in a single narrative.
- The more attentive you are to your dreams, the more your dreams will yield. You can grow more skilled at dream work. As you change and mature, your dream wisdom can yield even deeper levels of insight and inspiration.

As the examples in these chapters show, dream work can give you a decided advantage in relationships, problem-solving, decision-making, and overall life management. Look at your dreams as a dialogue between the life you're currently living and the one you're intended to live.

CHAPTER 4

Dream-Recall Techniques

"So I awoke, and behold it was a dream"

—John Bunyan

It's common not to have particularly strong dream recall. Many people report that they seldom or never remember their dreams. In many ways, this is like leaving $1,000 on your bedside table and forgetting to look for it in the morning. Since you know your dreams are there, taking a few simple steps to find them can be worth the effort.

In general, women seem to have better dream recall than men. This may be due in part to the physiology of a woman's brain, which includes more synapses connecting the two hemispheres. By having more connection between the "right brain" and "left brain," women have more access to the visual, memory, and inductive reasoning regions of the brain that seem to form dream narratives.

Men shouldn't think that dreams are unavailable to them, though, since many men regularly experience dream recall in addition to highly detailed dream narratives. Remember, structuring sleep for dream recall is a learnable skill.

Most important, keep in mind that dream recall is not "good" or "bad" based on the number of mornings you wake up with a clear dream recollection or vivid dream images. If you recall only one or two dreams a year but apply them constructively, you've had a good dream experience. Being receptive to remembering your dreams and applying the ones you experience and recall is the key to opening your life to the direction your soul wants to go.

Strategies to Improve Dream Recall

Here are some ways to carry dream experiences into your waking life.

Determine how long you are sleeping. Sleep moves in 90-minute cycles of falling into deep sleep, then moving into a REM cycle of about 15 minutes. REM sleep then repeats about every 90 minutes or so through the night.

Wake as close to (or even during) a REM cycle as possible. Waking after sleeping for six, seven, or even nine hours gives you the best chance of recalling your dreams.

Give yourself time to reflect on what was on your mind prior to waking. Often, you linger in bed for a few seconds and then must jump up immediately to shower, have breakfast, and start your day. Instead, let yourself awaken, but remain in a relaxed state for several minutes to seek the images that most recently filled your mind. It's not particularly hard to find a mental picture or relationship transaction that occurred in your sleep just moments before. From there, you can begin to expand your recall to remember why that image was in your mind and what preceded it.

Jot down the images and transactions. For many people, dream recall is easy in the initial moments after waking. Later in the day, however, when you are in a situation that requires input from your soul's wisdom, you have forgotten the previous night's dreams. The discipline of writing down dreams will help you recall them and eventually form a larger perspective on your dream themes and trigger events. Create a dream journal where you can store and treasure the contents of your soul.

OBSTACLES TO DREAM RECALL

Despite its implications in the spiritual dimensions of life, dreaming is very much a physical event, and various physical factors can limit dream recall.

- Cigarettes, alcohol, sleeping pills, certain prescription medications, and "recreational" drugs can all negatively affect the chemical environment for dream production in the brain.

- Eating fatty foods too close to bedtime distracts bodily resources away from the brain during sleep.

- Depression or anxiety disorders, and medications for these conditions, can create a chemical environment in the brain that affects dream recall.

- Untreated sleep disorders, such as sleep apnea, cause interruptions in the activity patterns of the heart, lungs, or brain during sleep and thus affect dreaming. Being overweight can worsen apnea.

CHAPTER 5

Disciplined Dream Incubation

You see things and you say "Why?"
But I dream things I have never seen and say "Why not?"
—George Bernard Shaw

et me sleep on it" is a common reply to a seemingly insoluble problem.
Often, this is a thinly veiled attempt to avoid or deny the reality of an
unpleasant situation. However, in bringing the power of dreams to the
challenges of waking life, the choice to "sleep on it" is often a wise one.

A significant exception to random trigger events is the discipline of dream
incubation. Disciplined dreamers can develop techniques for intentionally carrying
thoughts from the waking world into their dreams. The goal is to request the gift
of soul wisdom for the particular challenges faced by the dreamer in waking life.

Resources for Meaningful Dream Incubation

There are three tools that can help with the process: guided imagery, prayer or
meditation, and dream suggestion. To use any of them effectively, you need to
structure your bedtime routine around the goal of bringing your dream
resources to the problems of waking life.

Guided imagery is helpful for resolving nightmares. The goal of this technique is to form within your mind an image of the situation that needs to be resolved.

Dream Story: The Mystery of the Strange Man

A woman with a troubled past reported:

> *He's there again, the man I call the Mexican. He taunts me with his eyes, laughing at me and mocking me in my pain, saying nothing.*

DREAM COACHING

I suggested that she think about confronting "the Mexican." She should talk to him and chase him out of her dream. When she described the confrontation as she dreamed it, she said the Mexican seemed to shrink as she walked toward him. He became powerless! In order to accomplish this, she needed to think to herself as she fell asleep, "Tonight, I must confront the Mexican."

Parents can do this for children, too, although the technique differs somewhat. If a child has troubling dreams, parents can guide the imagery through bedtime stories structured around themes of love, affection, and stability. This process can be very helpful in creating a secure dream environment and in minimizing fear. Of course, you must also work on that goal throughout the waking day, not just that last 20 minutes before bedtime!

Prayer and meditation before bed are equally helpful in fostering meaningful dreams. Since your soul, the Divine-connected part of you, is the seedbed of your dreams, establishing a connection for personal growth and insight is an important dream development technique.

In dream suggestion, you can suggest to yourself the area of your life to which you want to bring dream resources.

- Remind yourself about the challenges of that day that are unresolved, and ask you inner wisdom to work on the problem while you sleep. Perhaps your marriage, your job, your parenting, or your friendships need to be reinvigorated.

- Invite yourself to dream of the life you have always hoped for, so that when you awaken tomorrow, you can begin building your waking life into the life of your dreams.

PREPARING TO RECEIVE DREAMS

Dream incubation techniques vary from culture to culture. This process can be used either to seek a dream for understanding or to understand a dream already received.

In the ancient temples of Zeus and Apollo, seekers developed dream incubation by entering into the temple after worship. They would spend up to nine days confined in a small cell, waiting for the gods to reveal their will. Native Americans practiced the vision quest as a form of dream incubation by going through a ritual cleansing, followed by a period of isolation in the wilderness. The Greeks' vigils in the temples and Native American vision quests have in common the act of deliberately preparing to receive spiritual intervention.

The Hebrew prophet Daniel spent three weeks incubating the interpretation of a dream, which came to him as another vision. It's difficult to discern whether Daniel's vision was a dream in the conventional understanding of the word, or some altered state of consciousness. The Hebrew words for "dream" and "vision" are used interchangeably in some passages, and Daniel himself referred to "my vision at night."

It's important to remember to be patient and receptive. Let the dream—and its meaning—come in its own time.

CHAPTER 6

Using Dreams to Improve
Your Life

*If one advances confidently in the directions of his dreams and
endeavors to live the life he has imagined, he will meet a success
unexpected in common hours.*

—Thoreau

You have a life, and you want it to work for you. In your day-to-day life,
you may be juggling household and work responsibilities, obligations
within relationships, the expectations of significant others, your duties
to yourself and your dreams, plus the need for exercise, recreation, and hobbies.
You have bills to pay, people to see, errands to run. Trying to create the space to
build a more fulfilling life in the midst of all of this can be downright daunting.

The pace seems never to slow down. And no one stops you to ask, "What
have you always dreamed of, and how can we help you achieve it?" More likely,
the people you see day to day are more concerned about making sure that *you*
meet the expectations they have of you, than they are with helping you craft a
life in alignment with your dreams.

You are the only one who can stand up for them. And it is essential that
you do, because this is what will bring you joy, and keep you energized and
healthy. A person without dreams feels hollow and is left to the mercy of the
devouring forces of the world. Your soul wants to express itself, rather than

submit meekly to the desires of the personality that would suffocate it. Your fondest dreams point you in the direction that will give you the greatest satisfaction. If you focus on those conscious dreams with enough intensity, your nighttime dreams will start dropping clues about the best way to accomplish what you want.

This is the only way you will achieve happiness. If you go after money, fame, or possessions just for the thrill of the pursuit, you're bound to come up short. Remember that rich people get divorced, file for bankruptcy, and lose control of their lives. Famous people have messed-up children. People who crave intensity become bored with reality. People with great knowledge about inanimate objects lack the capacity to connect with other human beings. Even the highest level of success can't protect you from unsatisfying outcomes in life.

Only when you put aside the pursuit of externals and begin working on developing the inner you will you begin to experience lasting satisfaction. Certainly, life on earth will never be perfect, but there are people who manage to create abundantly rich and deeply satisfying lives. One trait they have in common is that they are inner-directed. Another is that they possess sufficient willpower to keep working at it until they accomplish their goals.

Developing Your Inner Dream Coach

Today, people seek coaching in all kinds of arenas: sports, fitness, business, leadership, organizational skills. Typically, they pay premium prices for it. Meanwhile, the soul is perfectly willing to coach us for free, on a moment-to-moment as needed basis. We simply need to learn to attune ourselves to it. Being attentive to dreams is a great way to start.

Perhaps the best way to develop your inner dream coach is to record your dreams every morning. Use the tips I provide in Chapter 3, study the examples I've given you and try to approach your dreams in a similar fashion. As you become more comfortable, consider teaming up with a friend or joining a dream work group. Whether you work with a friend, a group, or just yourself, the most important thing is to keep practicing. With practice, your insight into your dreams and yourself will deepen, and yield information of inestimable practical value. The more you practice "receiving" the message, the more these messages become available.

The other key point is this: In dream coaching, as in soccer and other sports, there are boundaries. When you dream, you're working on your life alone and no one else's. You may be working on your response to, attraction to, anger at, passion for, or worry about others, as well as money you owe them or the control they wield over you—whatever. But the bottom line is that you must be reading this book for *yourself* for dream coaching to work.

This is hard for some people to understand. Often, when people come to me with a dream about another person, they expect that person to become whoever or whatever they were in relation to the dreamer in the dream. This may or may not happen. You can't make anyone else change, even if you dream of doing so. Your dreams are about what *you* expect, fear, desire, hate, need, want, or feel about life. They're all about *you*.

As you read, you can play a little game with yourself. Before you read the analyses of the dreams and how the dreamers applied the growth lessons, ponder what you would do if you experienced that dream. You can't use phrases such as "I would make my husband _____," because a dream is about *you*. Use terms such as "based on this dream, I would work on the _____ aspect of my life." This will help you develop your dream interpretation skills very quickly.

Dream Story: Using Dreams as a Compass

Dream wisdom is particularly useful to people who feel cast adrift, without direction. For them, dream wisdom can serve as a kind of compass, always pointing toward true North.

If the person you are today, fortunate in some circumstances and unlucky in others, is who you are ultimately meant to be, then true North moves every day. If, however, there is a "best possible you" that exists irrespective of whether today was a day of good fortune or not, then true North is always there to orient you in your journey through life.

In this following dream story, notice how the dream confronts the dreamer about his aimlessness:

John, a man in his early forties, recounted this dream:

I'm riding a train to the terminal. There is a briefcase on the tracks that I somehow know is full of money, and I know it's mine. The train I'm on is the wrong one and races past it. So I get off at the next terminal and get on another train. It again races past the briefcase. I get off but forget my belongings. I ride back to the station, but miss again. This cycle repeats half a dozen times until I wake up, feeling exhausted.

DREAM COACHING

After considering the dream, I asked him, "You have a difficult time making decisions, based on your fear of the outcome, don't you?"

"Well, with every decision I make, I seem to spend as much time regretting the other possible paths as I do pursuing the one I've chosen," he said.

Taking clues from the dream, I asked, "The harder you work, the less it seems to count?"

"I feel like I can work as hard as possible, as much as possible, but I won't attain the financial stability my family needs," he said.

The man's career wasn't going as planned. He felt opportunity had passed him by as he watched younger people achieve notably more success. Moreover, he was starting to doubt his ability to provide for his family. Trying to control what he could not, he started to become depressed.

He was at the stage in his life where he knew he was responsible for his growth and development as a person. We looked closely at his consistently getting on the wrong train in his dream. What were his criteria for choosing the train? He didn't have any. In waking life, what resources was he using to choose career opportunities? Basic instinct, he told me.

But the dream suggested that wasn't enough. He needed a "stationmaster," someone who could help him reflect on where "his trains" were going, rather than making one wrong trip after another. I suggested that he hire a personal coach and obtain other mentoring. That would give him the focus to engage in opportunities that brought him a higher return for his effort.

Through this dream, his soul lovingly showed him that "faster is not better: and that acting on instinct alone wouldn't get him where he hoped to grow." But the dream was encouraging over all, because it showed him he had the *potential* to earn good money, provided he maintain his focus with some help.

DOES DREAM INTERPRETATION CONFLICT WITH RELIGION?

As a Baptist minister, I'm well aware that the words "dreams," "Christian," and "pastor" are not often used in the same sentence, but I don't think they are incompatible concepts. By looking at the words individually, you can see their relationship clearly.

Dreams. For the first 4,800 years of recorded history, humans inextricably linked dreams to the sacred dimensions of being human. Dreams belonged to those who spoke to the spiritual dimensions of existence, whether priests, shamans, medicine men, seers, sages, prophets, imams, or spiritualists. Virtually all cultures have agreed that they can properly observe Transcendence through dreams.

In the grand scheme of things, it's more peculiar to say that dreams reside in the sphere of biology or (as Freud loved to say) empirical studies. The rigors of science have provided interesting insights into the study of dreams, but it's incorrect to constrain dreams to the confines of either the soft sciences of psychology and sociology or the biomedical realm.

Christian. The Judeo-Christian story presents about the same amount of dream literature as other faith traditions. "Organized religion" has responded more to the intellectual shift of modern Western culture than to biblical material with regard to intuitive ways of knowing. So, while many segments of organized religion reflect the current initiative to discard dreams, it's a result of neglect for the inner life of the person, not a mandate "not to dream."

In fact, dreams play a significant role in both the Hebrew Scriptures and the Christian New Testament. The patriarch Joseph relied on dreams to guide and preserve his life and the Egyptian culture. Joel saw dreams and visions as evidence of God's spirit within the people. Daniel interpreted dreams for the Babylonian kings to guide not only Israel but also the Persian Empire. St. Matthew's account of Christ's birth relates the use of dreams to direct the actions of the magi and the holy family.

Pastor. I am a connector or facilitator, not a psychologist, psychiatrist, biologist, or sociologist. What I hope to accomplish in life is to create and facilitate resources for people to connect with their innate divine spark, the soul.

I think about it each day. The same way a cancer researcher passionately pursues healing for the physical body, I ponder what makes a spiritual life healthy and whole. I crave breakthroughs in the "research" that will make such healing accessible to more people.

Thus, I consider it a privilege to journey with you into the dreamscapes of your life. Consider me your tour guide and companion. I hope I will point out scenes along the path of life that you may otherwise have missed, but I will do so with humility and as your fellow traveler.

CHAPTER 7

A Mainstream Approach to Dream Interpretation

Naturally, it should not be forgotten that no new dream theory could ever have seen the light of day had it not been preceded by the decisive, concrete observation of Freud, Adler, and Jung. Yet the dream theories of these pioneers led us astray.

—Medard Boss, psychologist and philosopher

The stereotype of the dream interpreter as an archeologist excavating the regressive corners of the psyche is a painfully inaccurate understanding of the work of the soul. I believe authentic dream work is forward thinking. The goal is to solve the problems of the real world. Adler called dreams "the interaction of the autonomous self with an autonomous world." The reality is that in waking life, you are more or less at the mercy of the power of the world. Dreams are a way to interact with the autonomous world to find your voice and power in it.

For most of human history, dream wisdom has been a revered and sought-after means of interpreting life. Four to five thousand years ago, Egyptian pharaohs slept in the temples, seeking revelations from the gods about the condition of the kingdom. The Hebrew Scriptures revered Joseph, the interpreter of dreams, as God's spokesperson in the late Bronze Period (about 1600 B.C.E.). In the latter prophets, the Hebrew words for "dream" and "vision" are used interchangeably.

The Greek philosophers, including Socrates, Homer, and Aristotle, wrestled with the purpose and meaning of dreams as human events. Native American spirituality held dreams in equally high esteem, pursuing the vision quest as the ordering principle by which life was rightly understood. Hindu spirituality appreciates the dream and a co-creative process with the Divine. Islam finds a voice for dreams in its spirituality as well.

For the first five thousand years of recorded history, dreams played a central role in the interpretation of human experience. What happened?

The Search for Meaning Goes Astray

Three patterns of thought emerged one after another, diluting the importance of intuitive knowledge. Each had its rightful place in the landscape of ideas, but none preserved or protected dream wisdom.

The first was the Renaissance. This period contributed much to the human story, but science moved to the forefront, sometimes to the exclusion of other, equally valid ways of knowing. The scientists of the era would weigh bodies as they died, trying to detect the departure of the soul. Unable to successfully measure the soul's presence, they questioned its existence, and its influence diminished.

Dream wisdom lost additional power when early psychoanalysts empirically studied the soul as an entity. Freud's obsession with the scientific method of understanding the mechanism of the soul worked against its very nature. When Freud combined his scientific method with his passionately held, even dogmatic, beliefs on the sexual theory of personality development, every facet of dream interpretation became an extension of the sexual identity of the dreamer. The result was that Freud, despite his significant contributions to psychology, alienated himself from the mainstream marketplace of ideas.

Carl Jung, the Swiss psychologist, tried to counter Freud's position by reclaiming the soul as an independent entity and the spiritual nature of emotional problems. He rejected the sexual theory of personality development. His position that an archetypal "self" governs the development of each person was revolutionary and important to the dream discussion. However, Jung died before he established an accessible theory of the role of dreams in the development of the soul.

The last undoing of dream wisdom in the mainstream came with the advent of the "Age of Aquarius" and subsequent New Age philosophies that disconnected dreams from real life in favor of categorizing them as an alternative form of reality. During this period, dreams were relegated to the periphery of contemporary thought and became more associated with astrology, tarot, and the paranormal than with development of the inner self.

The combined result of all these trends has, figuratively speaking, robbed us! Dreams are not gone, but you may feel "punished" for wanting to hear their wisdom more fully. You may feel that you can't listen to your dreams and be connected with reality. Or you may believe that because dreams aren't a measurable, "rational" experience, you're not entitled to invest them with any authority whatsoever.

The thing to remember is that dreams are a tool like any other. If you choose to use them correctly, they have the potential to help you build your life. If you apply them inappropriately, they can be as destructive as a bull in a china shop, offering lots of action but no benefit.

Since about 1980, there has been an emerging reaction to dreams as a soul experience by some in the medical community. They believe that seeking any latent dream content is a fool's expedition into the underbelly of the brain. The danger they observe is real, but their reaction is irrational.

Becoming detached from reality in order to chase images that exist only in your mind is called psychosis. Structuring each day around the content of your dreams, to the exclusion of other input, is indeed foolish and certainly not recommended! The goal is to solve problems in the real world, not create problems in it.

However, if you let the measurable experiences of life define your entire life, you lose something very precious to the human experience. In the theater of the mind, you may experience dreams that create feelings that are joyful, troubling, angry, envious, and so on. To discount and ignore the reality of that experience is to discard a real and unique part of yourself that you experienced in ways only slightly less real than if they had actually happened in waking life.

The place of dreams in your life is in the seat of self-observation. Rightly understood as a resource for personal insight, dreams help you begin to see yourself from perspectives not readily available in waking life. You can see how to leverage the strengths in your soul, how to protect yourself and others from your weaknesses, and how to build into your life the safety mechanisms necessary to protect yourself and others from the broken places in your self.

Like any tool, dreams are only as useful as the skills of the person using them. I hope you will use your dreams carefully, skillfully, and with an eye toward the wisdom they can impart into your life.

CHAPTER 8

The Biochemistry of Dreams

The findings of sleep research are interesting...even necessary. Not one of them brings us a single step closer to an explanation of dreaming as a mode of human existence.

—Medard Boss, psychologist and philosopher

Dreaming is a biomedical certainty. Often, the first protest about dream wisdom is, "I don't dream." But everyone dreams. It's more accurate to say that you have trouble recalling your dreams.

The human brain (and some research suggests the mammalian brain in general) is specifically designed for the dream experience physiologically defined as rapid eye movement, or REM, sleep. From our earliest days, we all dream. REM sleep was first discovered in the nursery of a large hospital in New York. Since that time, researchers have exhaustively studied the universal human pattern of sleep and dreaming.

Consider that all human brains share the capacity to dream. Regardless of whether we're a little smarter in book knowledge, common sense, or mechanical reasoning, or we possess greater ability in athletics, mathematics, or prose, we all dream. One reason is that each of us has a soul that hungers for growth and fulfillment through the human experience.

Not only is the capacity to dream inherent and universal, it's also a human necessity. We *must* dream. The accidental discovery of this fact came in the middle of the twentieth century, and the story is quite amusing.

At that time, in an effort to gain publicity, radio disc jockeys would participate in marathon broadcasts, in which they deprived themselves of sleep for days at a time. The result was that their brains went into REM-like frenzies during otherwise "conscious" periods. Hallucinations and impaired functioning in the "real" world accompanied these fits of brain activity, leading to the deduction that our brains have not only the *capacity* to dream but also the *need* to dream.

The Process of Dreaming

There are three major elements in the biophysical process of having a dream. The necessity of each element captures the beauty of being human. If any of the three were missing, it's doubtful that dreaming would be as enjoyable as it is.

Electrical environment. First, and not surprisingly, the electrical environment in the brain is more active during REM than during any other sleep period. In the general periods of restful and deep sleep, brain waves resemble a gentle ebb and flow of energy. However, the dreaming (REM) period features choppy shifts in activity in various regions of the brain that link emotions, vision, and memory to create a wave pattern that resembles waking life.

The dream period occurs during REM sleep. Indeed, as electrical activity stimulates the optic nerve near its receptors in the brain, the eye moves throughout its range of motion. A dreamer's eye movement during the REM cycle resembles that of someone driving in heavy traffic or watching multiple activities. The late David Maurice, Ph.D., of Columbia-Presbyterian Medical Center in New York City, believed that there's a highly practical side to this eye movement: The motion refreshes the oxygen level in the cornea.

Chemical environment. Second, the chemical environment of the brain undergoes noticeable shifts. Levels of the neurotransmitters serotonin and norepinephrine drop drastically.

The result is that while the electrical environment is escalating, the activity of the inhibition centers of the brain is receding because of an under-supply of their functioning resources. Simultaneously, another chemical, acetylcholine, washes through the brain stem in greater than usual amounts, activating internal memories and perceptions. (For a great discussion of the biology of the brain, see Pierce Howard's *The Owner's Manual for the Brain*.)

Sleep paralysis. Finally, there is the very unusual but highly practical phenomenon of sleep paralysis. What if your body had the capacity to enact every stimulus of your dream life? One night, while being pursued by dream strangers, you might awaken miles from home. Another night, while fighting off wild beasts, you might blacken the eye of your significant other. Dreaming would become a dreaded event for all involved.

In fact, your body is in a natural state of sedation while dreaming. In most cases, the REM cycle of sleep is the time when you are most still. Coming out of a vivid dream, you may feel the impulse to fluff your pillow or roll over to shake off a troubling image. Most of the time, however, dreams hold us in a nocturnal catatonia that protects our physical bodies while we exercise our souls and exorcise our shadows.

During lucid dreaming (see chapter 20), this sleep paralysis can be particularly troubling. Often, you feel unable to extricate yourself from the dream story as it unfolds or feel that your ability to react or defend yourself while dreaming is limited.

These physical characteristics of dreams are universal for all humans. Further, our physical necessity to dream is inherent and universal.

Isn't it fascinating that the human brain opens the windows of your soul through the physical event of dreaming? To deny a person (especially yourself) the ability to dream can do emotional as well as physical harm. People who are deprived of REM sleep may have trouble managing emotions, particularly anxiety, during waking life.

There are two factors that can interfere with healthy REM sleep.

- Alcohol and drugs that tamper with the chemical balance in your central nervous system can deplete brain chemistry and create dysfunction in the sleep centers. Likewise, some medications can overstimulate chemicals in the sleep centers, creating vivid dreaming.
- Unmanaged sleep disorders, such as sleep apnea, can upset your brain's natural capacity to rejuvenate itself through dreams.

Given the overwhelming evidence for the existence of and necessity for dreams in everyone, I hope you will begin looking more closely for yours.

CHAPTER 9

How Trigger Events Spark Dreams

Dreams are a natural and appropriate vehicle in which
the answers to prayers might be given.

—Edgar Cayce

Now you may be wondering, "Where do my dreams come from?" A short answer is, "From your inner motivation to experience a life that works." What all dreams have in common is a narrative that supports the soul's desire for health—your health. Your dreams represent your soul's bias toward seeking your well-being. The spark that animates your physical body has a desire to experience the optimal life available. Soul well-being includes healthy insight into your self as well as healthy and appropriate connections with others and the Divine.

However, there are identifiable ingredients that go into the mixture of images that construct a dream and play a role in its interpretation. Therefore, it's important to discern the overarching hunger for health as well as the specific issues that form a particular dream story.

Random Trigger Events

A trigger event is the first component of a dream scenario. Like the rolling snowball that starts an avalanche, a trigger event is any memory or experience that the psyche fixes on as the starting point of a dream. It can be innocuous or disconcerting, commonplace or unusual. Virtually every stimulus you have ever experienced can trigger your dreams.

A trigger event is like a pebble thrown into a still pond. The ripples move across the entire surface, bending the sunlight and shadows as they move, revealing and hiding what lies underneath. As the trigger event moves through your subconscious mind, it collects and displays sequences of images, many of which may be related in ways that defy easy explanation in waking life. As the chemical environment depletes the inhibition centers in the brain, images are created that may not logically fit together and may be troubling or graphic.

Every experience in your life places a potential trigger event into your mind. This is why dreams can offer you such a powerful growth resource— they are developed from within the full scope of your personal experience. The phenomenon of trigger events is also why you need dream guidance that is not simply content oriented. No one else has the same life content you do.

Trigger events can be literally anything that's in your brain. When you accept the reality that all of your relationship transactions, physical experiences, emotional memories, sensory stimuli, ambitions, and accomplishments are stored in your brain as potential trigger events, it becomes obvious that your ability to apply the power of your dreams to your life is essential. No one else can get "inside" you enough to do it for you.

Dream Story: Alligators in the Office

A typical mundane example of a trigger event comes from a man who recounted:

> I didn't sleep well last night. There were alligators in my dreams, crawling around the conference room, filling the office. It seemed like every dream I had included alligators.

Dream Meaning

Alligators had been a topic of conversation around the office that day, so it wasn't surprising that the dreamer's mind worked on that for a while during the night. The dream content itself was recreational rather than growth-oriented.

Dream Story: A "Bird-Girl" Is Threatened

The following example illustrates the "poetic" nature of some trigger events. A performance artist reported:

> *The bird-girl has just completed her transformation. A rough man comes along and lifts her by the neck. I have to threaten him to get him to put her down and back off.*

DREAM COACHING

At the time of this dream, the artist was involved in a new group that was starting to become successful. Shortly after the dream, however, one of the members quit to relocate, thus sabotaging any hope for future success.

In this case, the trigger event was quite subtle. Did the dreamer perceive a threat to the group, but without understanding where it would originate? The dream itself appears to be a mixture of warning and admonition for the dreamer to stand up for the aspirations of the group. Perhaps he intuitively felt the tentative commitment of his colleague and needed to be proactive to get those feelings into the open so they could be addressed.

When you recall a dream and begin to work with it, let the events of your waking life enter the conversation sooner rather than later. If you try too hard to work exclusively with the dream content, you'll miss the influence of events from your waking life that can help you interpret the dream.

Using "Parallels and Opposites" to Identify Trigger Events

To recognize waking events that trigger dreams, I use the rule of "parallels and opposites," which really is as simple as it sounds. Here are some suggestions.

Examine your dream content for what resembles and what dramatically differs from your waking life. If you dream in luxury but live with an empty wallet, the trigger event is your concern about your finances. If you live life concerned about being accepted by others, and your dreams are filled with pursuers, the trigger event is your need for affirmation.

Acknowledge that several trigger events may combine to form the narrative. For example, the bird-girl dream is interesting because of how it combines trigger events. Parallels and opposites influence the narrative of the dream.

- The group is becoming successful: The bird transforms into a woman or girl.
- The rough man comes along: Someone who doesn't appreciate the beauty of the group's success sabotages it.
- The dreamer has to threaten the man to get him to stop: Colleagues in waking life are antagonists in the dream.

Don't overlook the ability of trigger events to stimulate playful or recreational dreams. Some dreams are simply that, recreational experiences of your mind wishing to idealize fantasy experiences.

There's no predicting what will trigger your dream narratives. However, as your connection between your dreams and your waking life grows, you can develop skills in the discipline of dream incubation (see chapter 10). This is particularly useful for resolving troubling or recurring dreams.

Surprising Images

Regardless of whether the trigger events that spur your dreams are the random by-products of your life or the result of careful dream incubation, dream narratives can be full of unexplained surprises:

- Why does the car drive under water?
- How did the broken glass end up in the bathroom?
- Why did that bird turn into a girl?
- Why do things with very clear and defined roles in waking life possess new, illogical, and unusual powers?

• Why does everyone (or no one) help you?

The images, symbols, and transactions in your dreams are initiated by trigger events but reflect a variety of tools at work to relate the images to one another. Trigger events work within the superb system of your brain, finding and presenting the imagery of your life. Dreams work with you, a member of the human family, to design the story of being human. Finally, your soul connection with the Divine seeks meaning and understanding of that connection.

Thus, when you ask the question, "How did I get this person, place, or thing in my dream?" you are really asking, "What part of my life is this symbol connected with, and how?" In the 150 years of modern dream interpretation, people have written much about the origin of dream objects and characters, both familiar and strange.

The Principles of Condensation, Displacement, and Compensation

When dream objects and characters begin uniting to form a narrative, three primary instruments are at work in your mind to build the content. They are condensation, displacement, and compensation. We'll look at these concepts in more detail in chapter 8, but here's a brief description of each.

- *Condensation* describes how seemingly disparate emotions, memories, or abilities are related in the same object or person.
- *Displacement* occurs when a seemingly inappropriate object or person is placed in the context of a dream narrative. These first two ideas are among Freud's most compelling contributions to the field of dream interpretation.
- *Compensation*, identified by Carl Jung, is how you and others act, sometimes outside the boundaries of your waking ability, to function in the dream story. This is a very important dynamic to distinguish, because the way other dream characters compensate for you can reveal your weaknesses in waking life. For instance, if you're often powerless in dreams until a stranger comes to help, you're probably too dependent on others in waking life. If you often overpower others in dreams to get your way, you may be depending on control instead of relationship in your home life or elsewhere.

CHAPTER 10

How the Mind Weaves Dream Narratives

In a distempered dream, things and forms in themselves common and harmless inflict a terror of anguish.

—Samuel Taylor Coleridge

Condensation" and "displacement" are the two words that describe the sometimes hilarious, sometimes troubling, nature of objects and events in your dreams. Remember, trigger events can "bend" the clarity of conscious thought, relating objects and experiences in a way that defies easy explanation. As a result, what you often get in your dreams is a perspective not seen in waking life. "Compensation" describes the presence and actions of you and others in your dreams.

Condensation

Condensation occurs when one dream object is invested with abilities or properties it wouldn't have in waking life. Either an inanimate dream object or a dream character may be represented, as follows:

- The dream content may reveal or shroud the form of condensation. For example, a car drives under water as if it were on a dry road. The car is "condensed" into a submarine or amphibious vehicle. In another dream, a commonplace book is treated with sacred reverence.

- Condensation may invest a dream object with particular powers, depending upon who is holding it.
- An unknown person in your dream may combine the attributes of two or more acquaintances from your waking life into a single dream character.

Dream Story: A Dark Figure

A divorced woman reported dreaming:

In almost all my dreams, his dark figure is there, watching my every move.

Dream Meaning

In this particular case, the woman involved had been through a series of difficult relationships with men. The character in her dream was a condensation of her feelings and emotions about all the men in her life. Even in otherwise pleasant dreams, this "condensed" character was present, ready to thwart her happy plans.

Displacement

In dreams, displacement is the representation of one object or person for or as another. Forms of displacement can occur with you and any other person or thing. One of the most common forms of displacement is dreaming of yourself in a prior stage of your life. For example, you may be in your late twenties, but in your dream you're back in high school.

Dream Story: A Dreamer "Displaced"

A woman in her late twenties reported:

I'm the age I am now, but back in high school. All the people I knew in high school are there, and I begin yelling at all of them.

Dream Meaning

This kind of dream displaces the dreamer in order to give her authority over or more competence than the other characters in her dream. In this case, she yells at acquaintances who mistreated her during her teenage years.

Condensation and displacement are two dream phenomena that create the stereotype of a psychotherapist playing word-association games with a patient. In word association, the therapist's task is to relate seemingly disconnected parts of the patient's life to each other using dream content. The therapist tries to identify condensation and displacement in the patient's view of the world, using dreams as a primary resource.

Compensation

This principle is a little more difficult to grasp in the nuances of dream interpretation. Compensation describes the strengths and weaknesses of people in your dreams, including yourself. The following clues can help.

- Look at the expressions of compensation to compare who you are in waking and in dream life. Notice how they work within the rule of parallels and opposites to develop the dream interpretation.
- Other characters in your dream often have roles based on compensation for your personality strengths and weaknesses. Often, sages, shamans, guides, or elders give you the wisdom you need to understand your surroundings, find your way, or escape your captors in your dream. They compensate for deficits that you may perceive in your life, even if those deficits are not present in your waking life.
- A common compensation dream includes flying by personal levitation. Many flight dreams involve escaping troubling people or circumstances. In this instance, the act of flying compensates for the weakness of being unable to manage those people or circumstances through direct confrontation in waking life.

- Compensation is seldom delicate or discreet. Because we work hard in waking life to minimize our weaknesses, graphic dream narratives consequently force us to face situations in which our own lives are working against us. "Compensated" people who appear in dreams are often very repulsive or very attractive, or very powerful or very weak; you want to kill them or they try to kill you. When a dream character appears at one extreme or another, think about that person as a compensatory figure.
- Another form of compensation, which may be a little frightening, occurs when people who are close to you in waking life die in your dreams.

Dream Story: A Mother's Death

A woman preparing for her second marriage reported:

I have a dream that a large man attacks my mother, causing her death. I hear of her death over the phone, in my kitchen.

Dream Meaning

The largeness of the man was the key to interpreting this dream. In waking life, the dreamer's first marriage was undermined because her mother had remained the "largest" person in her life, even after the wedding. In fact, the dreamer continued to be contolled by her mother's expectations. The larger ego strength of her current fiancé needed to replace the disproportionate ego strength of her mother if this marriage was going to work.

D R E A M   C O A C H I N G

While this dream has a horrifying narrative, it has an inspirational message concerning the dreamer's growth as a person. In her first marriage, the relationship fell apart because of her unhealthy dependence on her mother and her mother's approval. As her second marriage approached, she could feel her relationship with her mother changing in her waking life. The dream affirmed that she needed to let those changes run their course so that her relationship with her husband could have the appropriate place in her life.

This dream illustrates compensation. It presents itself in strong terms because many times, we have very strong defense mechanisms that prevent us from seeing our weaknesses clearly. However, the dream told this woman in stark terms that her dependence on her mother must end in order for the planned marriage to thrive. Her soul called the dreamer to adjust her life to correct a weakness in her relationship style with her intended spouse. Once she realized that her husband-to-be was capable of meeting her needs for comfort in a nurturing way, her sense of intimacy in the relationship began to grow.

Secondary elaboration was also at work. The woman's initial reaction to the dream was fear of her mother's death, which illustrates secondary elaboration, the filtering of dreams through waking experiences. Such a response to dreams is natural but not necessarily accurate. In this example, the woman's secondary elaboration was that her mother *must* be about to die because of the dream.

A rule to remember is that in secondary elaboration, the personality, rather than the soul, is the dominant voice of the dream interpretation. Your personality interprets most of life as fears versus wants, while your soul interprets life as needs for growth.

An important facet of secondary elaboration is "reaction formation." As a child, you learned that touching a hot stove hurts, so now you pull away from potential burns. That is reaction formation. Much of your secondary elaboration has its roots in the waking-life reactions you've formed to images and ideas that are appealing, repulsive, and so on.

Strangers in the Night

Who are these unknown guys and gals who show up in your dreams and bring all forms of mayhem, romance, assistance, or conflict? Strangers can be any one of five possible representations.

The stranger is a part of you. This stranger often models for you a part of your life that you know is a weakness but that you haven't confronted. You're getting a lesson in which skills you need to develop to be more effective.

The stranger is a person you don't like, but someone you can't handle being disconnected from. For example, you may dislike your boss but need your job, or have conflict with a parent whose approval you seek. Then you may dream about a controlling stranger who makes you do things you despise.

The stranger is a person you are attracted to, but it would be improper to act on your feelings. Your dream gives you a safe target for those feelings. Usually, there is a particular physical feature or emotional characteristic that the stranger displays that is very similar to that of a person in your waking life.

The stranger is a wisdom figure. These are usually represented by older people who come along to guide you among several choices of action in the dream. Sometimes they wear ritual clothing, such as robes. If your mind casts someone from your waking world in a wisdom role, pay attention. That person may be in your life to help you complete the next stage of your journey.

Finally, strangers may be just that. They are simply background scenery to make the dreamscape complete.

To clarify a stranger's role in the dream narrative, ask yourself three questions:

• Do I interact with this person directly?
• Does the person develop the plot of the dream in significant ways?
• Does the person remind me of someone from my waking life?

PEELING AWAY DREAM LAYERS

A dream is a lot more like an onion than like an orange. Let me explain.

An orange has a peel on the outside, which you discard, and juicy fruit inside. Anyone can tell the fruit from the peel. Dreams are seldom so neat and orderly. Most of the time, they contain layers upon layers (like an onion), each of which is part of the whole.

An important dream that you had at age 25 may be recalled at age 35 or 45, with slightly new meanings and nuances that were not available to you 10 to 20 years earlier, but that now make perfect sense. Similarly, a dream may have a dominant meaning, but later it may provide subtle growth cues to examine other facets of life that weren't readily apparent the first time you applied the dream to your life.

The point is to avoid getting tunnel vision when you're seeking wisdom from your dreams. Even though I have categorized the dream stories in this book for readability, I struggled while doing so, because many of the dreams lend themselves to placement in three (or more) categories.

CHAPTER 11

Vivid and Lucid Dreams

We are near awakening when we dream that we dream

—Novalis

Almost as frustrating as poor dream recall is having particularly vivid dreams that remain stuck in your mind during your waking hours, yet you can't quite figure out what they mean. People who report vivid dreams are often highly perceptive, creative, visual people. They may have absolutely fascinating dream content that eludes ready interpretation, so they dismiss it too quickly as "just another crazy dream." Here is where a dream journal can be incredibly valuable.

While you're learning to see your dreams as valuable growth tools, hindsight is often the easiest way to interpret particularly vivid ones. However, once you become more comfortable with your soul's vocabulary of the trigger events that link your days with your dreams, you'll develop interpretation skills that provide more immediate insight. So go ahead and make some notes about even the craziest dream, then look at them that night to try to link some of the images of the dream with the experiences of the day.

Dream Story: A Vivid Recollection with a Life Message

A married mother of three reported:

I woke up completely convinced it was the last day of my life. I don't remember any of the dream images, but the dream seemed absolutely clear in that revelation. During my morning routine, I put my lipstick on very heavily and kissed each member of my family on the cheek. I did this so when they woke up and looked in the mirror that morning, they would know I loved them. That was more than 20 years ago.

Dream Meaning

The vividness of the dream troubled her, but the message she heard was one of beauty: "Tell your family how much you love them. Show them, let them see it."

Had she misunderstood the dream? Hardly. She understood it perfectly. To live a life of meaning, you must be connected with the people you love in ways they can recognize and experience.

Recalling Vivid Dreams

One frustrating aspect of particularly vivid dreams is deciding what to recall. Here are some suggestions.

Avoid overrecording the narrative. If keeping your dream journal becomes too cumbersome, you will quickly abandon it.

Focus on the objects you actually handle in the dream. Notice the colors and textures and how it felt to touch them.

Ignore the background. It's not important unless there's a big discrepancy between the object you're handling and the place you're handling it.

Dream Story: Doritos in the Communion Vessel

A woman in her early thirties with strong dream imagery reported:

I'm at church preparing to have communion. [She then elaborated on the details of the church in her dream, most of which corresponded to waking life.] However, when the elements are distributed to the congregation, I find Doritos in the sacred vessel.

Dream Meaning

While the vivid details of the dream confirmed the setting and locale of the events, the unusual presence of the Doritos interpreted the dream. The dreamer was on a spiritual journey in which she found unquestioning allegiance to the church hierarchy unsatisfying. As she moved away from the rigid formality of tradition, "having fun at church" often surprised her. Whereas in the past, church and clergy had seemed distant and unapproachable, they now appeared friendly and familiar. She often enjoyed but was also surprised by how comfortable she felt with the clergy.

SUDDENLY, I'M HAVING VIVID DREAMS!

Dreams can come in seasons. For months or years, you may experience very little dream recall, then suddenly find yourself in an onslaught of intense dreams. Many factors can influence how vividly you dream, including:

- A deeply moving emotional event, such as the death of a loved one
- Physical trauma, such as getting into a bad traffic accident, being robbed at knifepoint, getting mugged, getting shot, being physically or sexually abused
- Chronic stress, such as unrelenting exposure to combat, workplace pressure, or other hardships
- Beginning an exercise program
- Becoming pregnant (possibly because of additional hormone demands)
- Taking ginkgo biloba, St. John's wort, or other herbal or nutritional supplements

- Using certain antidepressants, anti-anxiety medications, or stop-smoking medications or patches
- Anticipating a significant life change, such as getting married, changing jobs, or buying a house.

Lucid Dreaming

Lucid dreaming is an interesting and sometimes troubling dream experience in which the demarcation between dreaming and waking is greatly obscured. In lucid dreams, your mind realizes that you're dreaming, yet surrenders its immediate connection with your physical body to allow the dream to unfold. As a result, you begin to "feel" the effects of your dream activities on your body. Moreover, you can begin to engage the dream and make choices about your actions while in it.

In a pleasant dream, this is wonderful. In the gray area of not being awake but being somewhat connected with your body, you can feel the warmth and euphoria of the story as it unfolds. However, the presence of natural sleep paralysis may cause very frightening sensations of being incapacitated during lucid dreaming. You may feel your inability to move and register it as a conscious physical experience in the midst of the dream state.

Dream Story: A Vivid Sensation of Dying

A 14-year-old boy reported the following:

I have been defending my home against an Asian army of some kind, perhaps Vietnamese. I am outnumbered and wounded repeatedly in the dream. A man comes up and shoots me in the head. I hear a sound. Suddenly I am aware that I am completely unable to move. I think to myself, "This is a dream," but I feel as though my spirit is preparing to leave my body in death. I am still unable to move, and I simply let myself continue to die. I feel the warmth of "blood" running down my face. I awaken fully, covered in perspiration and glad to be alive.

Dream Meaning

When the dreamer became aware that he couldn't move, his dream entered its lucid phase. The inability to command his body to move made his death in the dream more plausible and therefore more disturbing.

Indeed, being unable to move—sleep paralysis—is a by-product of sleep physiology. This phenomenon forms the foundation of what some people call the "out-of-body experience" or "astral projection," the disconnection of the conscious mind from the physical body. It can be a powerful way to experience your dreams and your life by allowing yourself to experience a mixed reality.

Dream Story: A Lucid Dream Appears Demonic

Some people perceive lucid dreaming as a demonic experience. A 36-year-old man recounted this distressing dream:

> *I am feeling physically oppressed and unable to move. My breathing is labored. There seems to be an all-pervasive darkness holding me down on my bed. I know that I'm dreaming, but I don't know how to extricate myself from the dream. Even my ability to speak has been impaired. Finally, I gasp the name "Jesus," and immediately I'm extricated from the breathless darkness of my dream and begin to focus on my bedroom, my wife, and my home. Eventually, I doze off, feeling as though I have just experienced something horrible.*

Dream Meaning

In this dream account, the physical suspension of the dream state becomes the context for the dream narrative. The result is frightening for the dreamer. Logically, the process makes sense. The mind works with the body: "If I can't move, there must be a reason. The reason is that it's dark and I can't summon the inner strength to move. Something has trapped me."

Lucid dreaming is not simply a spontaneous event. It is also learned awareness that dreamers can develop to inform and manipulate dream narratives. Once you've had the experience of lucid dreaming, you can "go lucid" during a dream. This is the process of reminding yourself that you are, in fact, in a dream state and therefore have access to creative resources greater than in your waking life.

People who experience recurrent nightmares often experience them as lucid dreams at some point in the resolution process. Being able to discern the dream as it's happening can allow you to be more proactive in directing, as opposed to simply experiencing, the dream narrative as it unfolds.

CHAPTER 12

Skillful Handling of Wish-Fulfillment Dreams

Dreams are the touchstones of our characters.

—Henry David Thoreau

Within the spectrum of your dream life, some dreams contain deep wisdom and possess the power to move your life forward in constructive ways, while others are essentially just playful and fun. They are both part of a healthy dream life, just as recreation is part of a balanced waking life.

Playful dreams are called "wish fulfillment" because they are simply that: Your brain and soul conspiring to fulfill some deep indulgent desires. Dreams about sex, money, and lifestyle, telling someone off, or meeting famous people are often wish-fulfillment dreams.

However, pursuing wish-fulfillment dreams with gusto and determination is a sure path to disaster, chaos, and dysfunction. The reason is simple: You will become the 3-year-old who wants ice cream for dinner, the 13-year-old who wants achievement without effort, the 23-year-old who wants accomplishment without experience, and the 33-year-old who wants relationship without responsibility, all rolled into one flawed, self-centered package.

Dream Story: A Pleasurable Tryst

A thirty-something woman reported:

> *I dream I have been intimate with my neighbor. He and I have run off somewhere together, usually somewhere tropical. When I awaken, I feel the warm flush of pleasure all over my body.*

Dream Meaning

The dream obviously has a strong sexual theme that the dreamer experiences with her body as well as in the visual dream narrative. The waking-life detail most important to understanding the dream is that her neighbor is a fashion model and fitness instructor.

Is there deeper interpretation material available? Certainly. How does this dream reflect on her marriage? Why does she seem to want or need the affirmation of being perceived as attractive by a much younger man? What about her contemplation of the consequences? Did her desire run unchecked by any responsibility to other relationships in her life?

Despite these other questions, the focal issue of the dream is the handsome younger man and the desire surrounding his physical presence.

While you sleep, your dreams indulge your playful imagination from time to time. Remember that every dream you recall may not have deep, life-altering meaning. Let yourself have fun while you grow!

FREUD'S THEORY OF WISH FULFILLMENT

Sigmund Freud believed that the content of dreams and what the dreamer wants out of life are inextricably linked. He was convinced that many dreams form from the unfulfilled wishes of childhood experiences. His theory arose from his own dreams following traumatic events in his childhood.

Freud was about five years old when his brother Julius was born. Like any firstborn child, he had enjoyed being the apple of his mother's eye until the baby came along. He later recalled feeling the resentment of being displaced. Tragically, Julius died when he was just eight months old. Freud felt a tremendous amount of guilt for his brother's death.

In another event a few years later, Freud lost control of his bladder in his parents' bedroom, earning him a stern reprimand from his father, who concluded, "That boy will never amount to anything." After that, Freud began to have dreams of achieving great notoriety and fame. He felt that these dreams, formed in reaction to the guilt and shame he felt about events of his childhood, were reflections of his inner wishes.

CHAPTER 13

Realizing the Power of Your Dreams

Hope is a waking dream

—Aristotle

I hope it's apparent to you that dreams are potentially very powerful. As the animating force of your life reveals guidance and wisdom for successful living, it would be foolhardy to ignore the advice.

The question is, "How do you begin to realize the power of your dreams?" For some people, this includes challenges related to recalling dreams. For others, dream recall is vivid, but comprehension is elusive. We will address both of these issues.

Regardless of what your particular challenges are, putting your dreams in their proper perspective is the first step in realizing their power in your life. Your dreams are among your most precious possessions. Within them, you can find:

- The truth about who you are and who you see yourself becoming in the world
- The answers you need to overcome some of the greatest obstacles in your life
- The dignity, joy, and excitement of what it's like to live as the person you are meant to be
- The creativity and potential to build your life into an expression of who

you have always wanted to be

• The resolution of how your life is supposed to work in the world.

That dream may be one of the few things in life that is truly yours. You must appreciate this reality before you can fully realize its potential. Since your dreams are intimate and personally revealing gifts of truth, it follows that they are worth an investment of your time and energy to maximize their value.

Once you accept that your dreams are precious gifts that are uniquely yours, it follows that you'll want to exert more effort to care for them. Think about your desk calendar for a moment. The business appointments, family obligations, and goals listed in it are, for the most part, meaningful only to you. Likewise, your dreams have value only to you, so you may as well work on bringing their power and potential to fruition.

PART II

How Dreams
Accelerate Growth

CHAPTER 14

A Universal Framework
for Growth

I've always had access to other worlds. We all do, because we all dream.
What I don't have access to is myself.

—Leonora Carrington, artist

Life interpretation, not dream interpretation, is the problem that plagues your waking world. Finding the right job, having a marriage that works, and building the internal structure to handle money effectively are issues that make or break life. Dreams are unique in their ability to motivate your growth toward the life you're meant to be living. To get there, however, you have to have some idea of what growth looks like as you experience it. For many people, the problem of dream interpretation isn't recalling the dream narrative; it's discerning what life is supposed to look like.

Four cornerstones to personal growth need to be in place for your life to move forward.

- The capacity for insight
- Connection with yourself, others, and the Divine
- The confidence to live in a world you can't control
- The creativity necessary to build and acquire resources for living

Without these four elements, growth is truncated or ceases altogether. As you become skilled at working with your dreams, you'll want to check your dream content against these four foundational growth principles to get the most thorough interpretations possible.

Your soul is an incredibly important resource toward this end. Because of its unique, life-animating energy, the soul has the capacity to guide you toward what life is supposed to look like. The challenge of most dreams is listening to the corrective impulses of the soul, some of which may be counterintuitive to waking life. This is because almost all experiences leave behind an emotional residue. If an experience is pleasant, you may be motivated to try to repeat it, regardless of whether or not it contributes to the overall health of your life. Likewise, you may continually avoid repeating unpleasant experiences, even if they're valuable for growth.

Dream Story: Multiple Wounds

A woman in her mid-thirties reported:

> I dream I am in a hospital with multiple gunshot wounds. The doctor caring for me seems very familiar, but is partially obscured by his mask. I think I should be dead, but the doctor is caring for me and doesn't seem worried about my mortality.

Dream Meaning

This dream is fascinating because, as I interviewed the dreamer, I found that the number of gunshot wounds corresponded exactly to the number of men she had loved in her life. The wounds were divided between head and abdomen, corresponding to her family connections and long-term dating relationships. The doctor, as it turned out, looked very much like a man she had recently started dating.

DREAM COACHING

The woman reported this dream at the outset of a new relationship that she perceived as potentially long term. However, she was struggling with ambivalence about the man and whether she should break up with him first, simply to avoid pain down the line.

Her soul was trying to tell her that the emotional residue of the past was impeding her experience in the present. She had not been damaged to the point of "death" in relationships, although she thought of herself as wounded beyond repair. Moreover, the "doctor" felt she was a desirable patient to work on, since he perceived her as very much alive.

After we discussed the dream, she allowed herself to relax and simply experience the relationship for what it was at that time, rather than pressuring herself to leave it or pressuring the man to commit to her.

The most common types of emotional residue involve addiction and avoidance of intimacy, both of which thwart growth.

- In addiction, people return again and again to familiar behaviors so they can avoid the discomfort of unfamiliarity with how to handle actual experience.
- By avoiding intimacy, people reinforce the many emotional wounds that stem from the isolation of feeling unlovable.

The soul has an inherent "homing beacon" that wants to move you toward growth, despite whatever aches and pains you have suffered. The problem is that the homing beacon may chart a course that calls you toward places that appear potentially painful.

For example, in the dream above, the woman was risking relationship with a man, and her emotional defenses were warning her that it might hurt. However, her soul was asking for the opportunity to experience feeling lovable to another person. The tension was obvious. While only time will tell if this man turns out to be her life partner, the only way the woman will ever have the possibility of marriage or life partnership is by taking a risk.

Finding the Soul's Well-Being

If you have a growth framework that clearly defines health and soul well-being, hearing the soul voice of your dreams becomes a lot easier. To understand what your dreams mean, you need to understand how your soul experiences well-being. The reason is obvious: Unless you can recognize your destination, it will be very difficult to know when you've arrived.

Dream content alone does not give full expression to the soul's well-being. For growth to happen, the dreamer must apply the lesson in waking life. Otherwise, there is no transformation. Interpreting your dreams but making no change in a less than satisfactory life would create yet another futile, broken part of life.

Do you feel that your life happens to you, or through you? In other words, do you react to circumstances and other people, or do you choose your actions toward them? Life is complicated, so the answer is not cut and dried. For example, poor health forces you to react to it, but you have choices in how you respond to the reality of being sick. One of the best gifts you can receive from dreams is clarity about what your choices in life really are.

What Clarifying Insight Looks Like

Clarifying your insight allows you to develop three important soul resources to optimize your character:

- Self-control
- Acceptance
- Follow-through.

These qualities form the foundation for growth because without them, your life will lack the inner resources necessary to achieve responsibility and causation in the world.

Self-control is the capacity to choose actions that offer the best good for yourself and others in a given situation. Self-control is more complicated than it sounds, because we often try to control others and lose control of ourselves in the process. Or we may try so hard to please others that we end up being controlled by them and lose control of ourselves.

Have you ever been in a relationship in which nothing you did was "enough" for the other person? Perhaps you even found yourself being angry with others because of the poor quality of your life in comparison to the seemingly better lives they were experiencing. This results from losing self-control. Most people around you are not trying to help you achieve healthy self-control. They want you to meet their expectations more urgently than they want you to achieve your goals. Consequently, self-control must emanate from within you.

This point about expectations is important for how self-control works in your relationships, too. It's unrealistic to want other people to meet your goals with the same urgency that you desire to achieve them. Instead of losing control of yourself as you try to "make" others live your life, you should work toward your life's dream apart from the need for others to make it for you.

Acceptance means living in the reality of now. Too often, our strong desire for life to be different makes us act as if it were. Psychologically, this is called "denial." Dreams may reveal wishes that long to be fulfilled, but the dreams that help you grow the most also teach you the reality of where you now are on the map of life in relation to where you want or need to be.

Follow-through means applying what you learn through insight to the discipline of living. Suppose I had a winning lottery ticket but was so busy planning how to spend the money that I never went to the lottery office and cashed it. That would qualify me as one of the stupidest people on the planet! Insight without follow-through is exactly the same.

Increase Your Connection

Humans are created for connection—no doubt about it. In order to feel good about ourselves, we need to feel that we fit in. Dreams can increase your connection in the three areas that matter most: your relationship with yourself, your relationships with others, and your relationship with the Divine.

Your relationship with yourself is interesting and important. Too often, we figure that what feels good to us or gains the attention of others must be good for us. Sometimes this is true.

However, feeling good can be a form of anesthesia. It prevents real feelings from coming to you. If you mask real feelings of hurt or loneliness with the anesthesia of doing what feels good, you'll lose the capacity to act for the good of the real you.

Many times you're so busy responding to others that you lose a basis for knowing yourself. Your aspirations get lost in a fog of others' demands. Then resentment begins, and your need to be connected with others for love and companionship morphs into controlling others with anger or sadness. Real relationships with others are lost once these toxic emotions take hold of your life and your soul.

You can reclaim *connection with others* when you choose to exercise your self-control in a way that lets you reach out to them without resenting their needs—by protecting yourself from being swallowed up by their desires. Connection is healthiest when others respect the limits of "no" within the context of "I'm here because I care."

Connection with the Divine means many things to different people. For you to be healthy spiritually, you have to connect with purposes and principles that exist outside yourself. Without this sense of connection, everyone around you will become an object to meet your desires, which again leads to a loss of self-control.

Connection with the Divine develops patience in character because you begin to see a world process at work outside yourself, to which you in turn contribute. The result is that you begin to see life more as a process than a series of events.

You can't overestimate the value of this experience! Once you understand that your life is a process, you can shift your perspective so that instead of focusing on what you want, you focus on what it takes to get what you want. Then you can concentrate on developing the personal skills and resources to attain it.

Strengthen Your Confidence

Healthy confidence is one of the greatest assets you can develop for personal growth. However, fear is often a primary motivating influence in our lives.

Some fear is good, because it reminds that some threats are real. Unhealthy fear paralyzes us and prevents us from completing the activities of daily life, let alone aspiring to the fullest expression of our potential.

All people, including you, do certain things and avoid doing others out of fear. We try to deny truth and to control reality to keep our fears in check. To function in life, an appropriate level of risk is necessary. Pursuing every experience with no regard for safety is a risk, but doing nothing and failing to pursue any opportunity is just as great a risk.

Dream Story: The Loss of a Pet

A married woman in her late thirties reported:

> *My friend gave me a dog. After I'd had her long enough to become truly attached to her, the friend came and asked to have her back.*

DREAM COACHING

The dream raised the question, "Is there a relationship you want to experience, but you're unsure that it will work out?"

"My husband and I are contemplating adoption," she said. "We're just not sure."

The dream was not prophetic, but it was asking the dreamer to carefully evaluate whether adoption was right for her family. Did she have the capacity for waiting and negotiating the possibly complex path to adoption, which could involve a relationship with another adult and eventually, her child?

In fact, after a few months of reflection, the woman and her husband decided not to pursue adoption. When they made this difficult choice, it was with the confidence and assurance that it was the right decision for them and their family. The family experienced a level of comfort and stability, and they chose not to expose it to the demands inherent in the adoption process.

This is in no way a critique of adoption (in fact, I am adopted). Rather, it's an affirmation that dream wisdom offered this woman, and all those who listen, insight that, when applied to life, gives us confidence in making decisions. There is no substitute for the inner peace that only the soul can provide.

Expand Your Creativity

Have you ever felt that your life needs a "'shot in the arm"? Does it need an elixir of some kind to renew its vitality? Life gets stale if you lack the means to be creative in the ways you parent your kids, connect in relationships, earn a living, and express your desires and aspirations.

Dream Story: A Mother and Child Bypass Obstacles

A mother of two in her early thirties reported this dream:

> *I am driving my car and go into a lake. I continue driving along the road. The people that drive toward me are very courteous, slowing down to make sure our cars have room to pass. The road ends, so I get out and start swimming with my youngest daughter on my hip. She seems happy with me. When I approach the water's edge, I look up and see my husband's coworkers cheering me on as I reach the shore.*

Dream Meaning

In the dream, the woman completed her journey despite obstacles and various modes of transport, even some types that seemed highly impractical in the waking world. In waking life, she was working part-time and raising two children as her husband pursued his career full-time. She enjoyed her life, even though it was demanding.

DREAM COACHING

The dream's clues led me to ask, "Even though it's overwhelming, you really love motherhood, don't you?"

"Being a mom is great, but I do feel the pressure to keep juggling my daughters' needs, supporting my husband emotionally, and doing my own work," she answered.

We talked about some of the ways she used her creativity to meet the demands of her life. She showed tremendous flexibility and resilience in the ways she pursued her day-to-day priorities. The dream was a gift empowering her to pursue her life in the ways that worked, regardless of whether it seemed right to others. Her creativity could work for her, and the dream affirmed that she should allow it to do so.

CHAPTER 15

How Dream Wisdom Can
Accelerate Healing

What surprises you if a dream taught me this wisdom... and even
if this should not happen, merely to dream it is enough.

—Pedro Calderon de la Barca

When dramatic gifts of truth from your soul emanate to the fore-front of your consciousness via your dreams, the logical question is, "What do I do with this?" Often, we treat dreams much like junk e-mail: We delete them without a second thought.

However, dreams can be an influential growth resource that fast-forwards facets of your life from mundane to meaningful—if you let yourself interact with them. Dreams can help you compare and contrast the life of your dreams with the one you are living.

In Asian spirituality, humans are endowed with a "third eye" that is a seat of will and spiritual insight. It also provides perspective and wisdom about what's going on inside you. Dreams can function like a third eye—a portal to perceptions of other dimensions—in your life, offering a perspective that's not possible in waking life.

Dream Story: A Kafkaesque Scenario

A 42-year-old man reported dreaming:

> *I am being interrogated by the authorities for a crime I did not commit. No matter how many forms of identification I provide, they refuse to believe who I am. Eventually, they start beating me, and I wake up.*

Dream Meaning

In this dream, the third eye pointed toward a facet of the man's life in which he feels he's not "acting like himself." Specifically, his use of Internet pornography was undermining his ability to connect with his wife and others. Although he had in fact not committed a crime, he felt that viewing pornography was inappropriate and was ashamed that he was doing it.

DREAM COACHING

The dream was a message from his soul to work on becoming an integrated, whole person rather than someone living two (or more) identities in a single life. This challenge both excited and frightened the man. He realized that growth and maturity (good things!) would be the inevitable outcome, but he also knew that facing the behavior and its consequences head-on could be uncomfortable.

This dream accelerated the growth process of developing integrity in the dreamer's life. It pointed to an area in which his behavior—which he thought of as "not hurting anyone"—was actually hurting him.

Once he quits trying to be who he is not, he will be free to work on who he really is. We'll look at this and other self-clarifying dreams again.

Dreams are a powerful, unique, and universal resource to accelerate your growth process. As you learn to receive their compelling gifts of truth uniquely tailored to your life, you can experience and accelerate the growth of virtually every facet of it. You can clarify your insight; strengthen your confidence; expand your creativity; increase your connection with yourself, others, and the Divine; and gain a host of other benefits.

To do this, the content of your dreams needs to enter the framework of growth. The results can be startling. As you begin to work on your dream recall and bring it to a growth-oriented agenda, you'll see your life from a perspective that has always been available but perhaps not acknowledged with the urgency it deserves.

If you've flown in an airplane, you have experienced the enhanced perspective that comes from changing your point of view. Once you take off, details gradually fade, but the higher you go, the easier it is to appreciate the overall landscape. You can see which areas are parched or fertile, urban or wilderness, land or water. Likewise, the act of dreaming gives you the ability to look at your story from a vantage point outside the possibilities of day-to-day living.

Putting Together the Puzzle of Life

Every experience in your life has put a puzzle piece, in the form of a dream trigger event, into your mind. You have this collection of pieces, but with no picture of the finished puzzle to guide you, you're virtually destined to build the picture that's most familiar to you, even if it's one you find undesirable. When you can fit the pieces properly into a framework and make an accurate picture, you will achieve growth in relationships and purposeful living.

Dreams are incredibly helpful in this regard because of the way they can help you see the boundaries of your life more clearly. Think about it for a moment. When you're working on a puzzle, one of the first things you do is find all the pieces that are straight on one edge. After you've put those together, you know that all the other pieces go somewhere inside. A framework to accelerate the growth process helps you join all your unique pieces to create the most desirable picture possible.

Jung's Theory of the Collective Soul

You need a design to know how the puzzle pieces go together. Carl Jung started working on this issue about 100 years ago, realizing that there is a best potential "you" that lives in contrast to your daily life.

His theory was that a collective soul (the psyche) lives beneath our conscious workaday world, guiding us toward fulfillment. The problem is that emotional pain; broken relationships with ourselves, others, and the Divine; and general human imperfection limit our understanding of who we are truly intended to be. One way to recover this truth is through dream wisdom that compensates for the brokenness we all inevitably experience.

Dream Story: Jung Sees Freud as "Waking Dead"

Jung learned a lesson through this dream:

> *I dreamt I saw Dr. Freud, although he was not dressed as himself. He was wearing the garments of a customs officer. His demeanor was as one of a waking dead person, sallow in appearance and feeble in his actions.*

Dream Meaning

After he had this dream, Jung realized that Freud's limitations were limiting him as well. Their relationship suffered, but as a result, Jung grew in his own right as a guiding light in the field of spiritually based psychotherapy. By listening to his dreams, he was able to overcome the fear of stating positions that were in conflict with Freud's. Even if doing so would cause their friendship to end, Jung realized that it was a risk he must take to grow as a person.

Your Soul Is the Key

The knowledge of the best possible "you" originates from the same place it informs, your soul. Your soul is the guardian of the vision you carry around of the person you were created to be. That vision wants to be found. Once found, it wants you to empower it so your life becomes fulfilling in ways that most deeply satiate your soul.

The conclusion is obvious: To work on accelerating your growth process, you need to work on your soul. Henry Cloud, Ph.D., one of the leading psychologists of our day, states the benefits in the following comparison: "There are two kinds of people in the world. The first are those who focus on what they want, but never get it. The second are those who focus on what it takes to obtain what they want and takes the necessary steps to achieve it."

Working on your soul puts you in the second group. Working on your soul with your dreams as a resource enables you to look at your life from multiple perspectives and thereby significantly accelerate your growth.

But what is soul growth? How can you tell if it's occurring? Simply stated, soul growth increases your capacity to function effectively in the world and meet your responsibilities. If you are growing in this dimension of yourself, life takes on a new aliveness. There's greater ease in your relationships and day-to-day affairs, which can give you a concrete example of what it means to "go with the flow."

Building Your Life

In order to build your life, you must begin to love yourself enough to care about where you end up in the world. In relationships, your life can be undermined by either of two tragedies. The first is needing the love of others so badly that you forget to care for yourself. The second is caring so much about the consequences of others' actions that you neglect the consequences of your own.

Either way, the result is the same: You will lose the capacity to love and be loved. Your dreams want to guide you to the place where you give meaning to life by both loving yourself in a healthy way and loving others for their benefit and yours.

You may be caught in the unfortunate trap of thinking, "It's only a dream." The way this trap works is simple but devastating. While dreaming, either in nocturnal REM sleep or daydreaming, you experience a life that works, a state of perception in which you readily discern the truth, overcome obstacles, or clearly identify protagonists. But rather than trust that intuitive guidance to direct you through the challenges of life toward the best expression of who you can be, you wake up, shrug, and say, "Oh well, it was just a dream."

Instead of seeing your dreams in contrast to your waking life, you can see them as a guide toward the life you are meant to live. By looking at your waking life and saying aloud for your benefit (and that of anyone else who cares to listen), "I've had a dream about a better life than I'm living right now. Starting today, I'm done discarding my dreams! Instead, I'm going to get serious about who I think I'm supposed to be in the world, and then go after it."

Such a confession helps bring your dreams to your waking life. It's a way of saying to yourself that when you get out of bed and approach the world today, it is with confidence that your soul wants to guide you, warn you, direct you, correct you, expose you, show you, lead you, and encourage you to find the best possible experience of who you can be. It's a great way to live, but at first, it will scare you to death!

This intimidation comes whenever you shift from discarding part of your life to taking responsibility for it. It is daunting to go on a diet, join a gym, decide to stop overspending, take responsibility for your loneliness, get out of a bad relationship, go back to school, change jobs, move, get married, or have a child.

It's also scary to visualize the possibility that your life can become more fulfilling. The reason is simple: Things can't get better unless you change.

Fortunately, bringing your waking life to your dreams and dream wisdom is a relatively safe change. Remember, your dreams are uniquely yours and intensely intimate. The challenge is not to turn yourself into someone you're not; rather, the challenge is to become the person you're really meant to be.

The Role of Dream Stories in Growth

Carl Jung, Joseph Campbell, James Hilman, and others have developed or built upon a school of psychology called "archetypal psychology." Basically, it says that cultures of the world have used stories, myths, and heroes to explain the human experience and its potential if it's navigated correctly. Whatever hurts inside of you hurts because it's tracking the "wrong" story or hasn't found the resolution in relation to what the Divine or God (in mythology, the gods) has designed to bring healing and restoration.

There's a lot of value in this way of looking at and understanding the human condition. As a child, you learned by hearing stories that were told to you. The stories became more complex as you got older, and you formed opinions from them about what was good or bad.

As you grew, you learned what parts of your own story were valuable to others and what parts they didn't hear or want to value. Many times, the grownups around you valued what made them feel good, even if it wasn't the part you liked best.

As an adult, you're building the story of what your life will mean to you and others. When your time with other people is over, they will think of what it meant to have you with them as the story of your life.

Building the Story of Your Life While Living It

Building your story is hard when you're actively living it. Waking life throws circumstances at us so quickly that coping with your immediate story undermines the story you want to develop. In dream wisdom, your soul shows you its experience of the story you're working on right now.

Some stories you like and others you don't, but all of them have something to say. And because they all come from your soul, they contain truth about you that needs to be understood and applied. Your soul is hungry to make your story that of a person connected to the Divine, others, and yourself in healthy ways that lead to effective living and a fulfilling life.

However, dreams neglect to denote for you exactly which wisdom they're showing you. It would be nice if each dream began with a title box, such as "This Is What You Should Do" or "This Is How a Person Is Overcontrolling You." You must conscientiously work with your dreams to optimize their benefit by developing discernment skills.

Dream Growth Comes When You See Your Life Story

To move from the person you are now to the person you are meant to be, you need to focus four aspects of dream wisdom onto your daily life. These aspects of dream wisdom derive from the reality that dreams show you truth from your soul. To get where you want to go, you have to know where you are, where you want to go, and what route will lead from point A to point Z, including all necessary points in between.

The four versions of truth represented by your dreams include:
- The life you're living (where you are on the map)
- Choices you should pursue (paths that lead where you want to go)
- The life you're living but shouldn't be (paths that lead somewhere else)
- The life you were meant to live (the destination)

These are the four kinds of truth essential for spiritual growth. Unless you have this information, life will always be a mystery.

The Universal Story of Being Human

Some of the stories in your dreams come from the universal story of being human. When Jung introduced the idea of a collective soul, he was saying that some of the human story is found in a universal script for all people in any age or culture. Often, these are the dreams that show you the points between where you are and where you want to go. If you were 5 feet tall as a teenager and grew to be 5 feet 6, you were 5 feet 3 somewhere in the process. It's a universal rule of growth.

The story of your dreams can help you find your way to the magnificent "you" that you thought could exist only in a fantasy world of your own making. You can't control all the variables life offers, but you can be more creative in your responses to them. You can't make other people treat you better, but you can bring the resources of your inner strength to your interpersonal relationships. You can't bring your dreams into your waking life, but you can bring your waking life into your dreams. Let me explain.

Once you wake up, the dream is over. However, your nocturnal experiences—the truths you were taught, the relationships you experienced, the sense of (dis)connection you felt to the grand scheme of your life, and countless others—leave a residue in your memory. As you awaken and walk through the world, the wisdom of your dream story can guide you. As you collect trigger events, your dreams will work with your accumulated experience to offer options for how you might use your resources and talents to continue making progress through life.

A Supercharged Growth Story

It doesn't happen every day, but in one of my dream cases, a dream came along that functioned in all four layers of truth for growth in a simple, elegant dream narrative.

Sheila, a twice-divorced mother, was in recovery from alcohol addiction and eating disorders. The trigger event was conflict over her mother's parenting style (her father was deceased). As I worked with Sheila, the excitement she felt as her dream taught her was evident in her voice.

Dream Story: A Mother's Refusal

Sheila redefined her life journey as a result of this dream:

> *I have grown a garden outside a home* [not hers in waking life, but the place she lived in the dream]. *My mother is inside the home. I want her to come out and see the garden, but she doesn't. It's upsetting to me, and I try to motivate her to come outside. She is unable or unwilling, and I feel very sad that I must enjoy my garden alone.*

Dream Meaning

In this dream, the dreamer's current location, need, growth passage, and ultimate destination were all discovered. As we consulted, I could feel the light bulbs go on in her head as she embraced new visions for her life and health in her soul.

Sheila was trying to rebuild her life in her mid-thirties. After being sober for several years, she was starting to see responsibility and creativity beginning to bear fruit in her life through employment and independent living. The responsibility she felt for her own life had brought her renewal and hope.

This is the home and garden in her dream. Her soul realized that she had the maturity to devote herself to goals for which the rewards require self-discipline and an ongoing commitment. The home was her independent life. The garden was her responsibility to nurture that life.

DREAM COACHING

Sheila's relationship with her mother was painful and complex. For years, she felt that her mother was unwilling or unable to affirm Sheila's autonomy as a person. Much of Sheila's acting out during her dysfunctional period was a way of calling her mother's attention to the pain she felt about her life.

In the dream, this was represented by the mother's inability to come out to see the garden. At first, Sheila employed an accusatory voice in the dream narrative and condemned her mother for not coming to look at her accomplishment. However, as she reflected on the dream narrative, she realized that her mother was somehow incapacitated during the dream and was unable, not simply unwilling, to come outside.

Dreams Can Show You Where You Are on the Map

Sheila saw her current situation in a new light. She realized that she was able to be responsible for herself rather than acting out against the pain she felt in her life. She also saw that her mother was more than simply unwilling or spiteful in resisting acknowledgment of her "garden." She realized that at some level, her mother was fundamentally unable to do so.

Dreams Can Show You Paths to Avoid

What Sheila's life was missing was parental affirmation. She and her father had a very complicated relationship prior to his death, and she had never felt that she was "enough" in his eyes. Her mother lacked the capacity to connect with her daughter's maturity, creativity, and autonomy in meaningful ways.

Children need emotional support and parental encouragement in order to become healthy adults. It's a rite of passage that helps us to see ourselves as no longer dependent children tied exclusively to the approval of our parents. In ancient cultures, a dying father conveyed a blessing to his eldest son, granting ascension to role of family patriarch.

Sheila's life lacked this rite of passage into adulthood. For 15 years since her first marriage, she had tried to fill the void created by feelings of disapproval she felt about the person she had become. In this particular dream, she very clearly saw the deficit in her relationships with her parents.

In the dream, she realized it was futile to try to coax her mother to recognize her accomplishments and creativity. In fact, continuing to pursue that goal was like pouring salt in a wound in her waking life. Her dream taught her that it was acceptable to give up on getting Mom's approval of her life.

Dreams Can Show You the Path to Growth

In the dream, Sheila had an experience that she had avoided in her waking life. "I feel very sad that I must enjoy my garden alone," she admitted. In waking life, her modus operandi was to try to exert enough power or conflict to control her mother's actions. Her acting out was a way for Sheila to get from her mother what she felt her mom resisted giving freely. She realized that she needed a healthy way to meet this need for affirmation and approval and that her alcoholism had been a way to mask the pain of not having them. Her relationships with men that feigned intimacy had been an effort to experience affirmation.

Sheila lets go in the dream. She grieves her mother's inability to come out and enjoy her accomplishments, but she doesn't neglect the garden because of it.

This dream revelation had a dramatic impact on Sheila's waking life. In the dream, Sheila saw a truth she had hidden from for years in her day-to-day living. In waking life, she constantly neglected her own life and responsibilities in an effort to get something from her mother that her mom couldn't give her.

In the dream, Sheila let herself go out and enjoy the garden alone.

Dreams Can Get You to Your Destination

To experience healing, Sheila realized she would need to bring other people into her life to support the grief she felt over her mother's inability/unwillingness to affirm her creativity.

One of the questions I asked Sheila in interpreting this dream was, "Who else in your life would you like to share your creativity with? Are there other people you would like to see your garden?" The list included her AA sponsor, an older woman who was a neighbor and mentor, her children, and several other supportive people.

The dream wisdom had shown Sheila the destination she needed to reach to experience better health in her soul. She had to accept that her mother, for whatever reasons, would not yield to Sheila's desire to experience motherly affirmation and encouragement. Sheila would instead allow herself to grieve that loss and find support in other relationships.

CHAPTER 16

Tools for Dream Analysis

There seems to be something in dream images that has a certain resemblance to the signs of language...that they mean something.

—Ludwig Wittgenstein, twentieth-century philosopher

S ince the goal of this book is dream processing for life development, you need to be equipped to interpret your own dreams in a growth-oriented framework. The possible symbols are too numerous to catalog and are connected so intimately with each person's life that they can't be generalized. Therefore, developing an interpretive framework is an inescapable task.

Since the interpretation of dreams is also the interpretation of life, it necessarily includes the dreamer's waking circumstances. As you'll quickly realize as you read the narratives, it's impossible to interpret dreams with integrity unless the goal of healthy, soulful living is in the forefront of the interpretation.

Dream Story: A Scene of Chaos

Susan, a married woman in her late thirties, reported dreaming:

I am back in my college workplace, but at my current age. It is chaos during the Christmas season. No one knows how to work the cash register, and customers are coming behind the counter. It seems that there a lot of mentally retarded people around. I ask my coworker what to do, and she replies, "We're on our own now." Her eyes have a deep blue hue, much more than in waking life. Finally, the two managers arrive, strangely unflustered by the condition of the store.

Dream Meaning

All dreams have the same components: a *context* (or environment), an *experience* or experiences, and an *ending*. There are often additional characters, but they don't necessarily have to be included. When they are present, they form part of the experience narrative. In this dream, all three elements are easily identified.

Context. The context was a workplace approximately 17 years in Susan's past. (An interview confirmed the inference of retail sales.) However, that's not all there was to the context discussion. Each aspect must be analyzed with equal attention to "the workplace."

The context was also defined by the season. In retail sales, Christmas is a make-or-break time of year, the season when it either works or it doesn't. The dream occurred about two months after Christmas, but it was a season in Susan's life that was a make-or-break period for her marriage.

The malfunctioning nature of the cash register was also a context element. It created tension because the store couldn't do what stores do—sell things. In reality, Susan's life "couldn't do" much of what she expected it to do. Hopes were constantly being deferred by malfunctions around her. These malfunctions were not within her influence, but she was being given an opportunity to structure her response to them.

"Chaos" in the narrative was another important feature of the context. It implied disarray and disorder. When I inquired what Susan meant, her elaboration was "there are customers walking behind the counter." This was a very important detail because in waking life, the counter is the boundary between the public and the employees. The dream was declaring that boundaries were being violated, threatening the structure of the dreamer's life.

Experience. The dream experiences address how the dreamer relates to other characters and her own feelings. In some dreams, this is the hardest part, because the visual context clouds what the dreamer does. Other times, the experiences are all individual, and there are no interactions with others. Nevertheless, the dreamer still experiences the dream.

In Susan's case, she not only observed but also experienced chaos. The loss of boundary between the customers and the employees could be potentially threatening. There are only few reasons why a customer goes behind the counter at a store, and robbery is high on the list. Other reasons could include the incompetence of the sales staff or disregard for the merchandise. Each of these three metaphors was present in Susan's waking life, as we'll see later.

Another prominent experience in the dream was the observation that many people in the store were retarded. Interactions with developmentally or physically disabled people are noteworthy in waking life due to either their level of accomplishment despite limitation or the profound level of limitation they reflect even in routine functioning. When people have notable disabilities, we experience that part of their lives in evocative ways that can run the gamut from admiration to revulsion.

Susan's exchange with the fellow employee was pivotal to the narrative. "We're on our own now," the coworker stated. Despite the inability to function, the loss of boundaries, and the mentally disabled customers, help was not forthcoming. The response had a very isolating, condemning effect on Susan as she recalled it.

The blueness of the other employee's eyes—much bluer than in waking life—was another experience of the dream. One of the first questions I asked before beginning interpretation was how Susan experienced "blue" in waking life. *For her, blue symbolized peace.*

The final experience in the dream was the two managers walking into the store. Unshaken by the disorder, they arrived without any fanfare or emotional response to the situation. It was almost as if they expected the condition of the store to be as it was.

Ending. A good movie is often determined by the quality of its ending. If the subplots are resolved and the protagonist is victorious, we deem the ending "good." Dreams don't abide by any such conventions of storytelling or structure. In this case, the narrative concluded once the managers entered the store and observed the condition of it.

Numerous conflicts in the dream story were unresolved. The chaos was still present, the cash register wasn't fixed, and there was no explanation of why the managers returned if the employees were "on their own." In this dream, the lack of resolution had a significant impact on the interpretation.

In every dream, one of the primary interpretation tools is to review what's complete and what's left unknown at the end of the dream. Taking an inventory of how experiences have been resolved or not can give significant insight about what parts of the dreamer's life have served as trigger events for the dream and how the soul perceives its progress in addressing and working through those issues.

One word of warning: Sometimes dreams end and begin with little or no intermission. Often, people who have rapidly shifting, seemingly disconnected dream scenes are trying to combine two or more dreams into a single narrative. Each time there is a change of scenery, there is a potential ending to the dream. Dream vignettes may be a series of images in a single dream, a collection of dreams commenting on a similar topic, or several dreams stacked on top of one another. Be sure not to presume too quickly how the dream ends.

Interpretation. Susan was experiencing fear and loss of control. I asked when she had been in a similar emotional place in her life. She stated that during college, she had gone through an emotionally fearful time, which she attempted to manage through physical intimacy. That had been her behavior pattern.

Now, during a critical period in her marriage, her husband's physical disability thwarted her expectations of marital intimacy. Other people were intervening, but some were dysfunctional themselves and therefore threatened to violate the boundaries of Susan's waking, married life. In particular, she perceived that one man's emotional development was so stunted that he was "spiritually retarded." While there may have been short-term gratification, the long-term implications were not appealing to her.

Susan sought solace during this difficult period by spending "mommy and me" days with her four-year-old son, on their own. Her son has radiant, sapphire blue eyes. The satisfaction she experienced as a mother gave her staying power for the period of her husband's disability and her subsequent disappointment in the marriage. In fact, she and her son functioned together in very fulfilling ways despite the chaos resulting from the family's current financial difficulties.

DREAM COACHING

Susan's soul was hungry for three things: relationship boundaries, healthy physical and emotional functioning in the marriage, and reassurance that perseverance was within her capacity.

Toward this end, I counseled her to monitor the influence of other emotionally dysfunctional people in her life. When you are in a lot of pain, other painful people seem more attractive. I also counseled her to break out of the isolation of her life by connecting more with other moms and their children.

In her relationship with her husband, the problem was twofold. First, the disability had affected virtually every facet of their relationship. Second, it was equally problematic that Susan (like all of us) carried a vision of "normal" in her mind, and whatever falls outside that vision is automatically "wrong." She needed a new "normal," based on the reality of her husband's recovery process rather than on her personal agenda.

This was indicated by the various chaos scenarios in the dream, followed by the coworker stating, "We're on our own." There really was no one else in Susan's life who could "make" her mate well or her marriage work better. The fact is that only she could address the situation directly.

The dream was about being proactive in the midst of chaos. When life is out of control, you can watch it flow by, or you can reposition yourself to find your voice within the chaos.

Two months later, Susan's entire family spent a week at the beach, seeking reconnection with one another, placing boundaries back in their lives with each other, and growing as a family. The dream didn't solve every problem confronting her, nor did the beach week return the couple to marital bliss. However, by listening to the wisdom in her dream, Susan was able to map out a proactive strategy for managing the stress of parenting, working, and living with a husband in recovery.

Often, this is what a dream tries to give you, the best strategy among thousands of possible choices. I encourage you to engage your dreams as a strategy-building tool to move toward the life you are meant to live.

COLLECTING DREAM MATERIAL

I once worked with a 40-year-old man who had the most remarkable dream recall I have ever witnessed. In his dream journal, he was able to include not only characters and events but also discrete background features of the dream scenes. In one dream, he recalled that the television (which didn't have a prominent role in the narrative) was tuned to the History Channel. This some-times worked to his disadvantage, however, as he obsessed over every detail in the narrative.

As you begin to collect your dream experiences, either through journaling or the spontaneous recall of particular dreams, here are several tips that will lead to stronger interpretation.

Don't make things more vivid than they are, but don't neglect the details that forthrightly represent themselves to you. If you recall that the car was red, record "the red car." If you don't know what the house looked like, but you know it was your house, leave the details speculative.

Be particularly aware of dreams in which you become lucid as they unfold. Lucid dreams (see chapter 11) offer an interesting glimpse of how waking emotions interact with soul representations. Specifically, the inability to act or the supernatural ability to face struggles in lucid dreaming can have an impact on interpretation. For example, you may be in a threatening circumstance and then think to yourself, "This is a dream, so I'm going to fly away" (from these people or this situation).

Don't obsess about every dream you have. You must experience repeated exposure to the hungers and motivations of the soul to become familiar with their cues and initiatives. Consequently, looking for a "magic bullet" each morning actually works against the very nature of the voice you're trying to hear.

The soul views growth organically, as a process that requires time to mature. Life is more like a sprouting seed, not a machine. Growth through your soul does not replace a broken part with a fixed one; it's a process of repairing over time. Being receptive is always preferable to being obsessive.

CHAPTER 17

Exploring the Interplay between Dreams and Life Events

How much there is in the Bible about dreams! There are, I think, some sixteen chapters in the Old Testament and four or five in the New in which dreams are mentioned, and there are many passages scattered throughout the book which refer to visions. If we believe the Bible, we must accept the fact that, in the old days, God and his angels came to humans in their sleep and made themselves known in dreams.

—Abraham Lincoln

If you reflect on all this, you'll see just how urgent it is for you to take responsibility for living the life of your dreams. There isn't a dream dictionary in the world that can truly guide you to the meaning of your life. Your soul can condense, displace, and compensate a thousand trigger experiences in a vast number of variations to give you the gift of precise truth uniquely catered to your life. Dream dictionaries with thousands of entries lack the one thing that's crucial to interpreting your dreams accurately: the experience of living your life.

The four basic ingredients of *trigger events, condensation, displacement,* and *compensation,* combined with the thousands of entries that form the visual and emotional memory bank of your mind, yield countless possibilities for dream narratives. While your brain is dreaming, the inhibition or self-control centers are dormant, and the neurotransmitter acetylcholine floods the brain stem, causing memories to flow together unchecked. Ten thousand dreams interpreted in a single book would only scratch the surface of the possibilities.

The results can be startling as imagery moves like a slide show through your mind. Indeed, many dreams reflect this physical reality as much as or more than they do any kind of psychological one. Because of this, some doctors are now downplaying the function of dreams as windows to deeper meaning.

However, when we recall dreams very clearly, we do so with the distinct impression that they must mean something. This has been the case for thousands of generations. Knowing about the biology of dreams is not the same as understanding their purpose or meaning.

Your Most Purposeful Dreams Come from the Soul's Hunger for Growth

Feelings such as disappointment, sadness, anger, and fear obscure the soul. Your soul wants to move toward a life that minimizes its experiences of negative feelings while optimizing its capacity for love and joy. This inner reality primarily motivates the dreams that mean the most to you.

Your soul constantly scans the possibilities of your life, looking for opportunities to move toward its optimal self. When you begin to interpret your own dreams for coaching and life development, the soul's specific growth motivations are central to the interpretive framework. Briefly, they are connection with yourself, connection with others, and connection with the Divine. Keeping these touchstones in place is essential to your dream interpretation. For example:

- The soul's inherent quest for growth often invests dreams with prophetic authority. You may experience a dream and then see your life moving in a similar direction. The soul, through its process of scanning possible outcomes and experiences, has prepared you for certain ones that it anticipates as likely.

- The soul may present a "good dream" that you hope your waking circumstances will begin to approximate. In this case, you begin orchestrating the circumstances of your waking life to get where the dream has enticed you to go.
- In contrast, a "bad dream" may present you with unsettling outcomes, and you begin to move your life away from circumstances that resemble the dream context.

If you ascribe prophetic content to such a dream, however, you may miss a growth message entirely, as dreams can (and most often do) fit a different interpretive context. While prophetic dream interpretation is appealing, it may at times be inaccurate. Not all dreams are prophetic, and we should not press them into prophetic interpretations to the exclusion of other options.

Dream Story: A Surprising Appearance

A startling but pointed example of a non-prophetic dream came from a single woman in her twenties who reported dreaming:

I am having an intensely pleasurable sexual experience. However, I open my eyes and see another woman.

Dream Meaning

The dreamer found the dream very alarming. Her experience and image of herself didn't include that possibility for her personal expression of sexuality. She immediately fixated on the possibility that she might become a lesbian at some point in the future.

In fact, she was enjoying her first mature adult relationship. A by-product of this was her increasing self-confidence as a sexual woman, and she was comfortable initiating that aspect of the relationship. This was a new experience for her, as her previous experiences had been immature and consisted of trying to satiate the desires of her boyfriends.

DREAM COACHING

Once she was assured that the dream wasn't an indicator of a future "change of teams," she relaxed significantly and gave herself permission to experience the truth of who she was. More important, she stopped experiencing her sexuality as a reaction to others' demands and recognized it as part of her life in which she could make choices, have control, and even say no when appropriate.

This dream connected the dreamer more completely to herself and her identity as a woman. To call it prophetic would have been to destabilize the health of her waking relationships as well as that of her soul wisdom.

Even when dreams do represent destabilizing scenarios, the goal is to stabilize the relationship environment of the soul. The key is to identify where the soul is scanning for identity in the midst of its relationship climate and see how the dream scenario points to a new, more stable situation in its resolution.

This is most frightening when a shift in identity creates a present crisis in the midst of hopes for future promise. The dreamer may be on the brink of some achievement or rite of passage into "the next level" of life. No matter how positive the change, however, it includes some loss of identity for the prior, less mature self. In such a situation, dreams often include visions of the dreamer's own death.

Dream Story: Dying in Her Dreams

A single woman in her late twenties recounted:

> *I keep dying in my dreams. I don't want to, but what's really upsetting is that I'm not that upset about dying. It's not like I'm committing suicide; I just seem to walk off the top of the building while everyone else is looking over the edge, or I step out into traffic, or whatever.*

117

Dream Meaning

At the time of the onset of these dreams, the dreamer was engaged to be married. She had functioned as an independent adult for about seven years and had developed a support system for that lifestyle.

The dream is about losing her most familiar identity to begin building a new one as a married person. If the marriage has any hope of lasting, she can't simultaneously be married and function as a single person. Her old way of relating to herself and others is "passing away."

DREAM COACHING

The dreamer was enthusiastic about the new relationship. The dreams were not frightening per se, except that she was worried that the glib attitude toward her own death reflected a major underlying neurosis. When I inquired about lifestyle changes that she had undergone or anticipated because of the marriage, however, she recounted quite a few.

She held deep convictions that a marriage should be a life partnership, and she was highly motivated to see hers succeed. She also realized that for this to happen, her old way of life would, rightfully, die.

Dream Story: Suicide

Another, more troubling dream came from an adolescent girl who reported:

> *I'm having dreams of trying to kill myself. I usually wake up before I get to try, but when I do try, it's a sure thing. What I'm doing to myself would work.*

Dream Meaning

This dream was doubly frightening because the dreamer knew she had a tendency toward depression. In fact, she had attempted suicide once. At the onset of this dream, her mother was very worried and sought intervention. Did this dream mean that her daughter was going to try to kill herself again?

It was the girl's senior year of high school, so I asked what she was afraid of. She discussed war, peace, hunger, and the global economy. I pressed again, "What are *you* afraid of?"

"I'm afraid of being on my own and messing up my life," she answered.

"How afraid?"

"I'm scared to death. I don't think I can handle the responsibility."

"Who can help?" I asked.

"I don't know," she said.

DREAM COACHING

We aren't designed to live in isolation like that. The person battling to find her place in the world might make great fiction, but it isn't reality. The reality is that we need others to mentor and encourage us as we move toward adulthood.

The girl's dream wasn't prophetic, but it was her soul issuing a call for help in the clearest terms possible. She needed a support system that could help her handle the responsibility that was coming her way. She needed connection that would help her find the character she needed to make it in the world.

Viewing the dream as developmental instead of prophetic, we see that the dreamer could find empowerment in two different facets of life. First, she knew she had to have constructive relationships with her mother and others. Her mom had an important role to play in developing the girl's self-esteem so she could feel competent to face the demands of young adulthood. Too often, young people treat relationships and friendships as optional, when they are anything but that.

When the young woman and her mother looked at the dream as a cue for growth in their relationship, they moved closer emotionally. In doing so, they took the most powerful step they could to prevent the girl's depression and a subsequent suicide attempt. Initially, when their dominant fear and paradigm were that the dream was prophetic, they lived in resigned isolation, dreading the inevitable.

Second, she learned to look her depression squarely in the eye. When you experience a part of yourself that you dislike, your first instinct is to hide from it, deny it, or pretend it doesn't bother you. Only when you let yourself confront something for what it is can you do anything to change its influence on your life.

You will begin to recognize patterns emerging as you build your dream recall and connect the narrative of your dreams with the trigger events of your day. You will see more clearly where your dreams are coming from and which trigger events cause which kinds of dreams for you. Even in very dissimilar dreams, you'll spot recurring characters who help you compensate for growth areas in your life. You will start to perceive an ever-emerging picture of your life, as you are and as you're meant to be.

PART III:

Understanding Different Types of Dreams

CHAPTER 18

Shame and Guilt Dreams

I do not understand the capricious lewdness of the sleeping mind.
—John Cheever, American author

S hame and guilt are two powerful emotions. Many of the choices we make in life are made to avoid shame or guilt. Guilt comes when you feel you should "do" or "think" to pursue. It arises when the reality of what you think, do, or say falls short of the person you think you should be. Many times, during waking life, a person devises complex rationalizations to avoid feeling guilty. However, honest guilt isn't the worst experience a person can have.

Shame is a toxic cousin to guilt. Most times, it occurs when a person has a legitimate need that is made into something "bad" by others. In the dreams that follow, the dreamers needed to be valued, comforted, and secure, but those needs were not validated in waking life. For example, if every time child seeks affirmation from his parents he is told to stop being a pest, the good thing he needs—love—is turned into a demand that he shouldn't expect other people to meet.

The soul wants you to accept responsibility for all your actions (good and bad). Moreover, the soul wants to absolve you of the toxic shame that comes when others unfairly place responsibility on you for their choices and actions.

Dream Story: A Violating Touch

A young man in his late twenties reported the following recurring dream from ages ten to twelve:

> *An alien has come into our home. It touches me on the genitals. My parents seem to know what has happened but haven't done anything to stop it. I'm angry with them for ignoring the situation. I wake up.*

Dream Meaning

The context was the home. It seemed to be reproduced in the dream according to the terms of waking life.

The primary experience was the violating touch from the alien. The secondary experience was the resentment toward the parents for not intervening. There was an implied time lapse as the dreamer internalized the experience with the alien while his parents did "nothing."

The ending of the dream was the man's unresolved anger toward his parents. The dream concluded with the anger hanging in midair, unexpressed but also unacknowledged.

DREAM COACHING

Of course, we investigated potential sexual abuse and eventually ruled it out. The man acknowledged that touching himself, as a boy, brought a feeling of comfort, but he also knew that his self-comforting angered his parents. Consequently, he felt very ashamed about his body and his thoughts about it. His father labeled the behavior as pre-homosexual acting out and frequently reminded his son that he would not tolerate a "fag" in the family.

This shame caused the dreamer to dissociate his touching in the dream. The anger he felt toward his parents for not intervening was really the anger he felt about not being appropriately comforted by his parents and therefore needing to comfort himself.

The dream was a way for the boy to resolve a catch-22. His impulse to self-comfort came from a void of feeling in his life, but by filling the void, he incurred shame and wrath from his parents. By not touching himself in the dream, he was emancipated from his parents' accusations. However, he was still able to express latent anger toward them for their condemnation.

For the man to grow through this experience, the dream gave him several developmental tasks. First, he had to grieve, rather than anesthetize, the lack of comfort he received from his parents. This was a hard task for an adult to grasp, let alone a child. But by saying, "I feel [scared-lonely-overwhelmed]" and enlisting parental support, he could ask for what he needed. Second, he had to learn not to feel guilty about needing comfort and feelings of security. Those needs are essential to the human condition. To deny them or manage them in isolation could have a long-term impact on his sexual development and capacity for relationships.

When the man clarified his emotions about how his parents, especially his father, reacted to him as a child, he began to connect more to his adult sexual identity. Instead of punishing himself for having needs, he allowed himself to acknowledge them and seek appropriate relationship support.

Dream Story: Identity Transformations

A single woman in her forties reported dreaming:

> *I experience myself as a donkey, being ridden by my parents. We stop for some ice cream. Then they dismount. The scene changes. We enter a library. As we do, I am transformed into a dog, an indistinct mutt. I defecate. Then I transform again into a beautiful Afghan hound with long white hair, exotic-looking and desirable. Next, I see an image of myself as a little girl, whole and happy. She notices that she has left her purse in the library, and she goes to retrieve it. I wake up.*

Dream Meaning

This kind of dream is interesting because the context and the experience were so interlaced. The context of being other than one's human self isn't particularly unusual in dreaming. Even morphing from one type of creature to another isn't completely out of the ordinary. However, the kind of animals the dreamer is or becomes forms much of the symbolic content for the dream and its interpretation.

The context of the dream was being these different creatures and what each one of them represented to the dreamer. The library was also a contextual component, reflecting to some extent the dreamer's waking vocation.

The experiences of being ridden, changing into two forms (mule to mutt and mutt to purebred), going inside a building, and defecating each moved the narrative forward and were relevant to the dream interpretation. Each experience was obviously important to the dreamer, as she had observable, visceral reactions to each animal form she assumed.

The dream ended immediately after the final transformation, without any return to interaction with her parents or others from waking life. However, it's noteworthy that the dream ended with the dreamer feeling exotic and desirable.

DREAM COACHING

In waking life, this dreamer was the younger of a set of twins, and she felt that her life lacked opportunity and support in comparison to her male twin. An emotionally distant mother exacerbated this situation. The dreamer perceived that she was the scapegoat who absorbed whatever exasperation her parents felt. Consequently, when she began to interpret the emotional experiences of her childhood, she often felt that her parents had burdened her unfairly.

The interview took an interesting turn concerning the first transformation.

The dreamer described herself as a mutt, "the kind you beat with a stick to make it go away." Often, when parental relationships are strained, the child grows into adulthood feeling isolated because her relationship with her parents was often one of isolation.

Defecation is an interesting symbol in this dream, as it appears to be the catalyst for the second transformation. In the library, she changes from burdened to isolated, but after defecating, she changes from isolated to desirable.

In waking life, this dreamer, like so many people, had to make peace with the pain she felt about the shame of being a scapegoat. Many times in life, we must exorcise our inner demons before our inner beauty can shine through.

The final transformation was equally visceral. The dreamer saw herself in a new way and cherished the new self very much.

The dream was a recounting and validation of her life. By entering the library, she entered her inner strength, unique from her sibling. Once she exorcised the shame she senses about herself in her parents' eyes, her transforming moment began. When the transformation was over, she was unique: No longer a beast of burden, she was then a highly desired member of a pedigreed breed.

Dream Story

A married woman in her early forties reported:

> *I am on the playground. I am a child, about eight years old. The turntable ride is going around faster and faster. I am enjoying it. A man I don't recognize is pushing it. He stops and walks away. I vomit on my yellow dress and am very sad.*

Dream Meaning

This dreamer reverted to a childhood age in the dream, so the events of her childhood were crucial to its interpretation.

The context of the playground was non-threatening, and the dreamer's activities didn't indicate sickness. She was able to participate appropriately in activities on the playground, and she had no dream illnesses or handicaps.

The merry-go-round spinning faster and faster was an experience of being out of control, but it didn't bother the dreamer. The experience of the man walking away precipitated the vomiting. After she threw up, sadness took hold.

The dream ended with the dreamer contemplating with remorse the condition of her yellow dress. Because the detail was included in the narrative, it was an important place to start my inquiry about the dream.

DREAM COACHING

I asked the woman, "What yellow dress did you have when you were eight years old?"

"It was a birthday present the summer my parents divorced," she said.

In fact, the woman had been one of the only children in her neighborhood to have divorced parents, and it pained her greatly. When her father left, she felt that her world had caved in around her. Having lost all sense of stability, she blamed herself, as children often do, for the failure of her parents' marriage.

As an adult looking back, she realized that guilt did not rightfully reside with her. However, as a child, the guilt had felt very real.

Common Elements in These Dreams

What all three of these dreams have in common is a physical manifestation of an emotional experience.

- Defecating and vomiting are by-products of a traumatic parental relationship.
- Being touched by a nonhuman is a way to be comforted without breaking the rules.
- In all three instances, the actions are a way of expelling the shame from the dreamer.

Shame is an incredibly destructive emotion from which the soul wants to protect you. It's also a futile emotion that leaves you fearing what you need, which is love. In each of these cases, it was not appropriate for the dreamers to feel as if they had to be "good enough" to merit love and comfort from their parents. The dreamers' parents didn't provide enough love and affirmation to allow their children to feel secure during the growth process.

When your dreams feature an experience in which you change your self-perception from bad to good or good to bad, recognize that as an important event.

Pay attention to every trigger event from your waking life and every detail in the dream to discern when you shifted your view of yourself in your waking life, and why.

The yellow dress was an important detail. It placed the dreamer in the time in her life when, as a result of adult actions, she felt outcast or ashamed. The woman who transformed into an exotic dog did so in the context of a library, which symbolized her arena of success in a vocation.

Guilt in Dreams

Guilty dreams come from feelings that should be acknowledged in waking life but are not, for whatever reason. Often, these dreams plague people who are rationalizing a waking life choice by viewing it as a necessary evil.

Dream Story: Multiple Marriages?

A marriage counseling client reported the following dream:

> *I am at my own wedding, marrying someone new. I haven't gotten a divorce; I'm just getting married again. I'm hoping no one will find out that I'm already married. Everything is going according to plan until my present spouse walks in the back of the church.*

Dream Meaning

In waking life, this client felt much anger toward his spouse and expressed it in a flirtatious lifestyle. He described the marriage as "abandoned" and used this to justify the flirting.

DREAM COACHING

In this case, the soul was asking for the marriage relationship to be resolved, one way or the other. Clarity brings health in relationships. As long as the dreamer continued his murky behavior, his marriage would remain ill as well.

CHAPTER 19

Prophetic Dreams

*Dreams are surely difficult and confusing and not everything in them is
brought to pass for mankind.*

—Homer

When people ask me to interpret their dreams, they usually want to
see their future more clearly. One of the most fascinating aspects
of dream life is the prophetic content that accompanies many
dreams. Sometimes this has to do with the way we use the word "dream" as a
synonym for "goal," "aspiration," or "achievement." One way to define
"dream" is as a form or structure that we use to interpret or build the future.

Many people expect that every dream they recall will contain revealed
future truth. This is the model of dream interpretation found in the ancient
Hebrew Scriptures when Joseph interpreted his dreams of leadership and in the
dreams of Pharaoh about the seven years of plenty and the seven years of
drought. The function of these dreams is to foretell the future.

Indeed, many dreams have some prophetic elements. Dreams really do
come true. The question is, "How?"

Recognizing Prophetic Content

To examine your dream for prophetic elements, look for one of three things:

- Revealed future truth

• Consequential truth

• Aspiration or inspiration truth that sparks deeper knowing.

Each of these three truths fits the definition of prophecy in a particular way that calls the soul to growth and maturity.

Revealed future truth is difficult to identify in dreams. It's easy to see where you've been once you get there, but it's difficult to anticipate what it will be like beforehand. The following dream story clearly illustrates this point.

Dream Story: A Prophecy?

A twenty-four year-old single woman related this dream:

I woke up with the number 120 prominent in my thoughts; I am concerned for my boyfriend, who is flying in to see me this weekend.

Dream Meaning

This was the only facet of the dream narrative the dreamer recalled. She was fully persuaded there was a premonition in the dream and was anxious that something might go wrong. Although her boyfriend's flight was subsequent to the terrorist attacks of 9/11/01, both he and she had flown on several occasions without anxiety.

DREAM COACHING

We went through the flight numbers for his trip, ages, dates, anniversaries in the relationship, and a host of other numeric variables, including additives, multiples, and divisors of calendar-related data. Given no other distinguishing attributes, I concluded that the number was an amount of money or a quantity of time, but not a harbinger of future doom. The dreamer didn't have any connections to 120 that made sense.

That weekend, their reunion went joyfully and as expected. However, the flight, Delta 5235 from Philadelphia to Cincinnati on April 11, 2003, was 1 hour and 20 minutes late departing from Philadelphia. Somehow the dreamer had perceived the numerals "1" and "20," even though she did not know what they meant.

Another form of prophetic dream prepares you for a journey through circumstances that are unavoidable. For example, a reality of life is that all people are mortal and therefore temporary. An equally important reality is that we all grow up. People are not always there to meet our needs. The soul is hungry to put these and other truths into our awareness. However, internalizing these realities and living with them is far different from intellectually agreeing with them.

Consequential truth in dreams illuminates the effects of certain events in waking life. Because this type of dream gives the dreamer an opportunity to foresee the outcome of situations more clearly, even in experiential ways, it is prophetic. The message is potent because it allows you to "experience" the effects of certain actions through the mediation of the soul rather than through the direct experience of waking life. This can be a huge benefit in terms of warning you away from danger or helping you gain skills for handling forthcoming challenges in waking life.

Dream Story: Seeing the End?

A woman in her late twenties reported the following dream. At the time, her grandmother was terminally ill with cancer and was getting worse.

> *In my dream, I am in the house and everything is the same as in real life. I get out of bed, but then I get scared and jump back in the bed, hiding under the covers. I look at the edge of the bed and see a child's doll that scares me. The bedroom door opens and I see my dog. I look at her eyes, and they are really scary. She disappears. Then I see my cat, and her eyes are a scary black with a cloudy, glassy look. All I can think of is a demon. All through my dream, I feel strange, weak, as if I'm drugged.*

She continued, "Then I woke up. I was in the bedroom, feeling really creepy. I got up for real, went into the living room, and lay on the floor. Then

I felt strange again and went back to the bedroom. I tried to think happy thoughts, but the dream haunted me, and the eyes of the animals and the doll. I was so scared that I couldn't stand it anymore and ran to my parents' bedroom and asked my mom if I could sleep in their bed. Even when I was little, I never slept in my parents' bed because of a nightmare. My parents were puzzled, and my dad ended up sleeping in the hospital bed."

The dreamer also reported, "A few months later my grandmother was hospitalized—she was living her last days. They kept her on morphine, and her eyes looked exactly like the eyes I saw in my dream that night."

Dream Meaning

This dream gave structure to what the future might hold. Obviously, the presence of the hospital bed confronted the woman with her grandmother's prognosis in very stark terms. It was the end of her time on Earth with the dreamer.

DREAM COACHING

Prophetic dreams can help prepare you for experiences that you are going to work through or help others through. This is a great example. Since the woman was part of the caregiving team for her grandmother, she was being prepared to comfort her during her illness and the effects of treatment.

One of the most effective caregiving skills a person can develop is empathy with a suffering person. This dream gave the dreamer an experience that would help her identify with the struggles her grandmother faced during the last days of her life. As a gift from her soul, it was also a gift to her loved one.

LINCOLN'S PROPHETIC DREAM

President Abraham Lincoln had one of the most spine-chilling prophetic dreams in history. Presidential biographer and personal friend Ward Lamon Hill reported the following, which the president shared with him about 10 days prior to his assassination.

Lincoln dreamed of hearing the sound of mourners throughout the White House. In his dream, he rose from his bed and wandered through the White House, looking for the source of the sounds. Every room was lit, but empty. Eventually, he walked into the East Room and found an honor guard keeping watch over a casket, with mourners gathered around. Lincoln inquired of the soldier, "Who is it?" The soldier replied, "It is the president, sir."

This dream leaves many unanswered questions: Did Lincoln intuitively discern the plot hatched by John Wilkes Booth and others to take his life? Did he "know" that certain Confederate sympathizers, angered by their inability to win the war, would strike at him personally? Was Lincoln given a gift of divine insight to prepare himself for coming events?

Not every dream is prophetic. Dreams like this make it plain that some have insights into the future that defy ready explanation. The question Scrooge asks the ghost of Christmas Yet-to-Come in *A Christmas Carol* is a good one to ask yourself: "Are these the things that must happen, or the things that may happen?"

CHAPTER 20

Entrapment Dreams

Unfortunately, the balance of nature decrees that a super-abundance of dreams is paid for by a growing potential for nightmares.

—Peter Ustinov, British actor

Dreams of being trapped are often very troubling. The soul has an inherent desire for autonomy and accomplishment. When the dynamics of your waking life work against these qualities, your soul will actively seek to represent them to you through dreams.

The context issue is the primary feature of entrapment dreams. Houses, prisons, museums, vehicles that the dreamer can't control—all can be symbols of containment or entrapment. There is usually only one "container" for the entire dream narrative.

The identifier here is the dreamer's recognition of choices and control in the dream narrative. Not every dream of a house involves entrapment, because many dreams let you leave the place at will. "Don't want to" and "won't" are different from "can't." The first two imply voluntarily staying in the place, the latter the inability to leave. Pay close attention to your recollection and recording of this part of the narrative.

Dream Story: Locked in a Cabin

Sarah, a single woman in her twenties, reported dreaming:

> *My boyfriend has built a cabin in the woods and locks me in it. My libido is running very hot. He calls on my cell phone and chastises me for wanting/needing to release this energy.*

Dream Meaning

In this dream, someone else has inflicted entrapment upon the dreamer. Even though Sarah wanted to leave, she couldn't. The location of the cabin "in the woods" was important to the overall interpretation of the dream. It gave the narrative an implied isolation from others, designed not by Sarah but by her boyfriend. He isolated her, implying some shame on his part for her behavior. She was not only trapped, she was also hidden.

DREAM COACHING

In waking life, Sarah was much more self-confident in physically expressing her affection than her boyfriend was. I asked if her boyfriend's mother was very religious, and she stated that his mother was a non-practicing clergyperson. In fact, his parents learned that Sarah felt comfortable about having sex with her boyfriend and severely condemned their son for choosing to be in relationship with her.

When I asked Sarah about her boyfriend's reasons for adopting his parents' viewpoint, she replied, "He doesn't want me to taint his experience with his future wife." The boyfriend felt that until he was entitled to experience all of his sexuality, he could have none. Thus, he attempted in waking life to isolate his sexual experience from other aspects of his relationship. Obviously, that is a poor relationship strategy.

In the dream, Sarah was unable to extricate herself from the cabin but maintained a link with the outside world via the cell phone her boyfriend used to call her. The boyfriend's waking pattern was to try to isolate Sarah from his mother, who didn't see eye-to-eye on their sexual relationship and many other topics. However, he also wanted to stay connected with his girlfriend. The wireless link of the cell phone is a perfect metaphor for the nature of their relationship under the influence of his mother's (rather than his own) desires.

In working with the dream, Sarah realized very quickly that the relationship would be profoundly strained if her boyfriend lacked the capacity to act as his own person. For relationships to bear the fruit of maturity, such as marriage, the commitment between the man and woman must eventually become superior to their commitment to their families. While Sarah was willing to do this, her significant other was not.

The two of them were at different places in their ability to express and experience their needs. The role of libido in this dream represented Sarah being adult about an aspect of her life that the boyfriend allowed his parents to control. Sarah's desire to express her sexuality and the boyfriend's chastisement over the phone to prevent it mirrored the waking experience of the relationship.

In terms of soul growth, Sarah had two options. She could either wait for her boyfriend to recognize and validate her needs in the relationship, or she could seek a new relationship that validates them. Either way, she had a proactive role to play.

Sarah's soul didn't want to surrender the proactive position. Sometimes it's tempting to think, "Well, I can live without this part of the relationship," but that is the gateway to losing yourself in someone else's needs and expectations. Psychologically speaking, we call that "codependence."

The Message of Entrapment Dreams

In dreams where you feel trapped, the message is to find resources that you can bring to your life circumstances to move forward. People who have recurrent entrapment dreams often perceive themselves as powerless in their waking life. Consequently, they stay locked up.

However, Sarah had one very obvious choice: to stay in the relationship, or not. After she had this dream, she could see clearly what the cost of either choice would be, and she could choose decisively from an empowered position.

Power against Entrapment

This is a slightly different type of dream. Here, the autonomy of the soul is protected (unlike the above example), but the cost of exercising that autonomy confronts the dreamer.

When you exercise your power, it costs you something, and it costs the people you stand up to as well. Even in a loving relationship such as husband-wife or parent-child, when one party asserts autonomy, both (the one asserting and the one asserted upon) lose some emotional capital.

For example, part of becoming mature is becoming a person independent of your parents, and the goal of parenting is to raise independent, responsible children. However, separating yourself from the identity your parents desire for you can be complex.

Dream Story: Breaking Free

Phil, a single man in his early twenties, reported dreaming:

> *I am completing a jump [for military training.] The hatch is closing before I can get out of the plane, and I use my hands to break through the fuselage.*

Dream Meaning

Obviously, you can't jump out of a plane if the doors are closed, so this counted as an entrapment narrative. However, unlike Sarah, who stayed entrapped, Phil exercised brute strength against his captor (the plane).

DREAM COACHING

In waking life, Phil was in the military and completing jump school at the time of the dream. My first question was, "How is your mother handling your military career aspirations?" I suspected they were putting quite a strain on the relationship, which he readily confirmed.

In the dream, Phil physically forced his way out of the plane, despite significant bleeding and pain in his hands. In waking life, sleep deprivation had lessened the effects of sleep paralysis, and he had torn down a ceiling light fixture in his barracks, bloodied himself, and required several stitches in his hands.

Phil's soul wanted to experience competence as a soldier and as a man, confident in his own ability, master of his fears, and so on. However, experiencing that aspect of himself would require a painful separation from the identity his mother desired for him, as opposed to who he wanted to become. He didn't want to experience less love toward his mother, but he correctly realized that he couldn't allow her desires to control his heartfelt aspirations as a soldier.

Interpretation Guidelines

In waking life, one of the things that entrap us most is the expectations of others. When people around you communicate their disappointment with your choices or limit them because of their expectations, you may dream of feeling trapped.

The context of an entrapment dream may point to one or two expectation conflicts in the dreamer's life. For example, the plane in the previous dream was the conflict point between Phil and his mother. His desire to conquer his fears and develop his military career conflicted with her expectations. In Sarah's dream of being locked in a cabin, her entrapment represented the conflict between her desires, her boyfriend's, and his parents'.

The key is to identify the significant relationships in waking life that are "stuck" or experiencing a conflict that seems irresolvable. The soul hungers to move through the conflicted situation toward greater well-being. Thus, you can look at the dream content to discern what your choices are.

When you analyze which way your (or another dreamer's) waking choices show an outcome bias for the conflict, you begin to see whether the dreamer is pursuing growth or avoidance.

- Phil had already decided to embark on a military career. Therefore, the dream was confirming that rather than avoiding the cost of that decision, he should accept a certain amount of pain. He didn't need to retreat from either his career goals or his relationship with his mother, but he could expect some bumps along the way.

- Sarah had her dream literally a day or two after some disconcerting events with her boyfriend and his family. The dream was oriented toward sorting out the ambivalence she felt about staying in the relationship (even though she wasn't fully connected) or abandoning it. Another possibility she faced was that there could have been some truth in her boyfriend's mother's analysis of the relationship. Even though Sarah disagreed, she was of the same faith and wanted to be thought of as "good."

PLACES YOU CAN'T LEAVE

In dreams, there are innumerable places where you can get stuck, unable to exit. In dreams I have listened to, read about, or had personally, the places people have been trapped include apartment buildings, churches, houses, the underworld (à la Tolkien's *The Hobbit*), giant mushrooms, museums, jails, prisoner of war camps, cruise ships, and so on.

When you encounter a dream (yours or someone else's) of being trapped in a place, here are some clues to the meaning:

- Lack of an exit can be a form of oppression. The dreamer understands that he must leave, and the inability to do so creates conflict or anxiety, or exposes the dreamer to the dangers that lurk within the place.

- Other times, the way to exit is simply a mystery that the dreamer lacks the ability to solve. There is no "mission" to leave the place, and no one else in the dream can accomplish it either.

- The initial question should always be, "Where is this person's life getting swallowed up by the expectations of another person?"

• The first place to look is at the mother-child relationship. One of the early tasks of maturity is realizing that a mother wants different things for a child than the child wants. As you grow up, you have more opportunities to experience conflict between your desires and your mother's.

• After mother-child relationships, other relationship conflicts emerge that involve your desires and those of your peers, people you date, your employer, your partner, your spouse, and eventually even your children, if life takes you in that direction. (What goes around comes around!)

The point is this: Being trapped often signifies an expectation conflict, and the place you are trapped often provides a clue about whose expectations are conflicted. I always start with the earliest relationship—the parent-child relationship—and work forward.

CHAPTER 21

Recurring Dreams

There couldn't be a society of people who didn't dream.
They'd be dead in two weeks.

—William Burroughs, American author

Recurring dreams can take many shapes and forms. Often, they seem to begin and then resolve very mysteriously. One night, a particular dream will be your constant companion, and then it evaporates. This can go on for hours, days, or years.

The onset of the recurring dream is one of the primary interpretive tools for discerning its meaning, since recurrent dreams originate with a particular trigger event. An office conversation, a TV show, or a vivid movie may germinate images that repeat throughout your dreams that night. Other times, an unmanageable experience causes the soul to raise a warning flag that further growth will be limited until the experience is resolved.

As messages from your soul, recurring dreams reinforce the importance of making progress toward a fulfilling life. When a dream recurs over an extended period of time, it indicates that your inner self is being traumatized, paralyzed, or otherwise rendered unable to resolve a particular growth issue.

In addition, the context and experiences of a recurring dream play the most significant role in interpretation. This is because the dream has no real "ending." If it did, it wouldn't be recurrent! Even dreams with unresolved storylines end in a way that allows the message of the soul to complete its work.

In recurring dreams, however, the dreamer intuitively knows that the end exists outside the experience of the dream. This usually indicates that the dreamer's inner self has not yet presented the best resolution possible. Such dreams may be a by-product of trauma, which by definition is a level of pain or conflict that is beyond the ability of the body's coping mechanisms to process.

Sometimes physical trauma can trigger a recurring dream. Post-traumatic stress disorder as a result of a near-death experience frequently causes this kind of dreaming.

Dream Story: A Soldier Relives Being Shot

A veteran of the Vietnam War reported this recurring dream:

I am dreaming of the day I was shot. I seldom actually get shot in the dream, although sometimes I do. Most often, I recognize the danger and start yelling for others to get to safety.

Dream Meaning

The former soldier's recurrent dream increased in frequency around the weekly and annual anniversaries of the date when he was shot; it occurred most often on Thursdays and during the anniversary month. Because the dream operated in a traumatized aspect of the dreamer's life, the normal pattern of sleep paralysis was often absent. Many times, the dreamer would push and struggle to get to safety or wander around the house in the dream state. As troubling as it was, the dreamer and his wife accepted the reality of it. Guiding the dreamer to the bathroom and awakening him was sufficient to resolve the dream for that evening.

The long-term issues associated with this kind of post-traumatic stress disorder can be very difficult to resolve. Sleep and psychological trauma specialists have tried all manner of interventions for this type of dream. The success of these treatments varies widely.

The soul is not a physical being that can be traumatized, but it undergoes experiences that are traumatic to personality. Usually, these traumas exist in one of three dimensions: connection with yourself, others, or the Divine.

Dream Story: Witnessing a Tragedy

Emotional trauma is just as difficult to manage as physical trauma. A teenage girl reported dreaming:

> *I am running through the woods. I hear a young woman crying in pain. She is being beaten. Sometimes I just see her wanting me to help, but other times she is me. Sometimes I am running toward her and feel myself being chased.*

Dream Meaning

This dream stemmed from the tragic murder of her half-sister at the hands of a serial killer. The death occurred at a time in the dreamer's life when she was old enough to understand what death was but too young to comprehend tragedy or randomness in life. Indeed, many adults, as well as children, find it hard to comprehend difficult events such as random killings.

As a young person, she saw how these events had an impact on her father and other family members. As she observed their difficulty in processing what had happened to the murdered sister, she realized that she lacked the resources to absorb the experience. The magnitude of the event was like trying to get 20 gallons of water into a 2-gallon bucket. The result: The water simply overflows.

The girl needed structured grieving time to learn to process the emotions. This was complicated by her father's resistance to grief-intervention counseling. As long as he was not consciously processing the pain, he continued to project inordinate anxiety for the well-being of his surviving children, which assured their continued pain.

Dream Story: Protecting a Treasure Box

Another recurrent dream is from a teenage girl, who reported:

> *I am running through the woods carrying a small box. It is very impor-
> tant to me, like a treasure or keepsake box. There are people chasing me,
> who I don't see in the dream or know as being part of my real life. They
> want the little box. It's my job to protect it.*

Dream Meaning

In the secret life of children, there is often a treasure that's completely and
uniquely their own. My own children have gone through the ritual of collect-
ing odds and ends to create a treasure intimately connected with their inner
world. It's a reflection of the soul exercise of becoming a soul unto yourself.

For this dreamer, the small box was more significant than that. As an
adopted child, she (as I and all other adopted people do) had been learning
to comprehend the disconnection between her family identity and her biological identity. There was literally an identity in her that was not available
to her or reflected by anyone around her. No matter how vigorously she
pursued it, it wouldn't be found or captured.

Another facet of this recurring dream may have revolved around her
commitment to purity before marriage. As a teenage girl, she was starting to
be pursued by young suitors, not all of whom held the same convictions as she.

DREAM COACHING

This dream wasn't particularly painful for the dreamer to experience, so
resolving it wasn't an issue. The wisdom coaching was to monitor her waking life and think about who was trying to get close to her and for what reasons.

When she had the dream, I suggested she look for cues from her waking life that pointed to one of three interpretations:

- Was she developing a secret treasure in her heart that wasn't ready for
  public consumption? This could include an aspiration, a goal, or a

secret longing.

- Was she confronting questions about her biological family and what they might be like? Heredity is a common topic in middle school and high school biology classes; friends who knew of her adopted status might ask if she ever wondered about her "other family." Doctors who dealt with her as a young adult would ask the inevitable family history questions, to which she couldn't provide useful answers.
- Was she was being asked to give part of herself to a responsibility, a relationship, or affection in ways for which she didn't feel ready?

All of these are developmental tasks that teenagers experience, so it was normal to experience a little reservation when facing these challenges.

CHAPTER 22

Identity Dreams

I dream, therefore I exist.

—J. August Strindberg, Swedish dramatist

One of the most important and recurrent questions in life is "Who am I?" As we change over time, so does the answer to this question. The demands on and responsibilities of 5-year-old children are much different than those of 25-year-old and 50-year-old adults.

Carl Jung was a leading spokesperson for the idea of an archetypal journey that defines how we experience the aging process. He believed that dreams could play an important role in how we identify the internal resources (emotional resources and competency) to cope with the expectations and demands of aging.

Psychologist authors James Hilman, Joseph Campbell, Thomas Moore, and others have looked at mythology, ancient literature, and legends to see how these archetypes were expressed in common throughout humankind. They also observed that humans go through emotional stress when passing from childhood to adolescence to adulthood, and that adults have certain tasks to complete at approximate ages in their twenties, forties, and eighties.

Many times, the soul and personality wage a tug of war to discern how, given a change in life circumstances, a dreamer should perceive a new identity. These include issues as diverse as personal responsibility, familial relationships, and sexual orientation.

Dream Story: A House without a Wall

A 17-year-old girl reported this dream:

I am in a house out in the desert, but one side of the house is missing. There are butterflies all around me. The scene keeps changing from regular desert to beautifully painted landscape in a metallic hue. I wake up.

Dream Meaning

The dreamer is this case was moving to a new home, far away from some bad memories. In addition, the move was creating opportunities for her to function more as an independent adult and less as a daughter dependent upon her mother (her custodial parent). At age 17, this would be expected, as the daughter was taking on more adult responsibility, appearance, and relationships. This image was captured in the house with the missing wall.

Homes are often symbols of mother power. However, the partial home indicated the renegotiation of that relationship, and the wall missing signified new opportunities to experience life on her own terms.

It's important to note that the dream didn't happen "out in the desert" but "in a home in the desert." While the dreamer was shifting in the mother-daughter relationship, she was not abandoning it. The house was there, but it was less restrictive than if all four walls had been present.

The butterflies were symbols of both socialization and transformation. The dreamer didn't simply observe the butterflies, she interacted with them. By adopting their graceful style, she could fit in with them. She also saw herself as transforming, much as butterflies are transformed creatures. She not only wanted but needed to be less dependent. She perceived that butterflies, by virtue of their ability to fly, have more options for action than caterpillars. She felt herself becoming a healthier person as a result of the move and new independence.

DREAM COACHING

The young woman was coached to move into independence slowly. Sometimes parents isolate their children abruptly at a given age, or the children isolate themselves. The dream was an encouragement to stay connected with Mom while exploring life on the dreamer's own terms. By socializing with the other "butterflies" but still having access to the sheltered place, the dreamer could appreciate the beauty of her transformation more fully.

Clarifying Identity in Other Ways

Dreams can clarify identity in less poetic, more graphic ways as well. Many times in dreams, we kill people or cover up dead people. Most of the time, this is not a latent desire to commit a crime! Rather, it's a way to rid ourselves of a habit or identity that we feel is inappropriate to our life circumstances.

Dream Story: Disposing of a Body

A woman in her late teens recalled a disturbing dream that recurred throughout her first two years of college:

> *I have found a young girl's body. I didn't kill her, but it's my job to dispose of her remains. I put her in the floorboards of my flat. I'm not particularly repulsed by the task.* [In waking life, she was more repulsed by her calm demeanor in the dream.]

Dream Meaning

The context of the dream was the dreamer's college apartment, which corresponded to her waking-life college dwelling. The experiences of the dream were encountering the dead girl, feeling compelled to dispose of her remains, and beginning to do so. The lack of feeling about the task in the dream was a notable aspect of the narrative. The dream concluded as the body was hidden.

DREAM COACHING

The recurrence of the dream during a transitional time in the dreamer's life was important. Many college-age people are acutely aware of their need to put away childish habits. In addition, college typically involves early experiences with alcohol and sexual relationships. Often, as the transformation from child to adult unfolds in waking life, there is a latent desire to punish whatever childish insecurities may rear their ugly heads. The dreamer was acutely aware of these life passages and her response to them.

Aspiration Dreams

This type of prophetic dream helps you shape what you want out of life. The soul has cues about what life is and what will most suit your growth and maturity as a person. This type of dream is particularly helpful because you can compare two or more aspirations to determine the best structure for you.

Dream Story: Fame versus the Fiancé

A man relayed a dream that his fiancée reported:

> *My fiancée has a desire to become famous. She dreamed she was at a pop concert. The singer picked her out of all the people to go up on stage with him, so she did. Later, she met him backstage and kissed him. I was at home in the dream, and she started going out with the star. They got quite intimate; they took off their clothes in front of each other.* [This was something she found very hard to do, even in front of him, because she was so self-conscious.] *Later in the dream, she rang me to come over to her, so I got a plane over and met her. She told me then that she had to choose between us. The pop star said he would give her the life she dreamed of, the life of fame. In the end, she chose me, and she flew home on the plane.*

The man stated that flying was his dream, but his fiancée was very afraid of it and would find it very hard to get on a plane. She was also afraid of his becoming a pilot. Then he asked, "This was her dream, but what does it all mean?"

Dream Meaning

The dream was about the woman comparing two major life aspirations and clarifying her commitment to the relationship in marriage versus an entertainment career. In this dream, she was comparing two possible outcomes for her life. Prophetically speaking, the dream indicated that the relationship will move forward and the couple will marry as planned.

DREAM COACHING

I intuited the man's concern: "You're wondering about the marriage, right?"

"Well," he admitted, "the part about her taking her clothes off gets under my skin."

I counseled him not to be worried, that she was falling in love with the idea of spending the rest of her life with him.

However, the man was concerned that perhaps the intervening elements in the dream also had prophetic material in them. At first, he was very undone by the dreamer getting undressed in front of the singer/celebrity. He was equally concerned that his beloved was able to work through her waking life fears so readily with a complete stranger in the dream setting.

It's important to note that the singer wasn't a known person from the waking world, but rather a creation of the dreamer's subconscious. The singer was an "everyman" representation. Dreams often use this form of condensation, placing a stranger in a prominent role so there isn't a bias toward a particular waking-life attachment.

This condensation changed the dreamer's basis for the experience element of interpretation significantly. There wasn't a competing image of substance, just contrast. I told the man that I thought he was the pop star in the dream, and that I hoped he realized how much his fiancée loved him. Although the "taking off their clothes" part was probably what he found most troubling, that and the flying were two of the more profound gestures in the dream. His fiancée saw herself becoming who she was really meant to be in life through her relationship with him, and that it was better than her aspiration of being a pop star!

Understanding Your Ability to Function in Certain Roles

Life is a continuous negotiation among the various roles we fill. For example, a woman who chooses not to have a career outside the home will generally have a greater capacity for childrearing than a woman who chooses to divide her attention between both endeavors.

Dream Story: An Option Revealed

A mother of two young children was considering having another child instead of returning to work. She reported dreaming:

> *I am driving, with my children in the van, through a dangerous neighborhood. In spite of the dangerous surroundings, there are water slides along either side of the road. I'm lost. I see a mother playing with her small child and stop to ask her for directions. When I finish speaking with her and turn away, she stabs me in the back with a hypodermic needle.*

Dream Meaning

The context had two parts, being in the family car and driving in a dangerous neighborhood. Both elements were important to the dream interpretation. The van was a place in which the dreamer felt safe and in control. However, the environment outside the van was threatening and unfamiliar. The water slides were a peculiar feature not common to waking life.

The experiences revolved around fear of being lost, interacting with the stranger, and being stabbed. The first two are commonplace experiences; almost everyone has felt the nervousness of being lost and the need to rely on the guidance of an unknown person. However, being stabbed in the back with a hypodermic needle by an assailant who otherwise projected goodwill and seemed nonthreatening was troubling. The dreamer recalled that in the dream, she decided to approach the other woman because she was apparently a mother.

The ending of the dream is unresolved. There was no motive given for the attack, no response on the part of the dreamer, and no treatment of the wound. Many times, a dream with a startling ending causes the dreamer to awaken rather than to inquire what comes next.

DREAM COACHING

When I started to work with the dream, my first intuition was concerning childbearing. "Are you ambivalent about having a third child?" I asked.

In fact, the dreamer was eager to be pregnant and experience delivery, but she was overwhelmed by the logistics of actually raising a third child. Moreover, her husband was in a very demanding career, which meant that from 6:00 a.m. until 7:00 p.m., she functioned as a single mother.

The growth coaching from this dream revolved around her need to experience healthy connection with her desires and personal capacity. Many times, we're infatuated with part of an experience but ignore the troubling facets of it. By paying attention to her dream, she began to resolve her desire to experience pregnancy with the reality of childrearing responsibilities. She allowed herself to appreciate her other two children more fully as she made peace with what was best for herself and her family circumstances.

Dream Story: Sexual Identity

A young man who was considering a change in sexual orientation reported this dream after an initial discussion of his readiness to pursue this course:

I'm sitting in a church service honoring men. One by one, the men are standing up and shouting, "I'm a man." The women respond to this with, "And a good-looking one, too!" When my turn comes, I stand up and do my

thing, but there is no response, just silence. I hear a chuckle or two. I sit
down, and a young woman [a peer, of dating age] puts her head on my
shoulder in a loving way. The scene changes, and I'm in medical school.

DREAM COACHING

The question arose, "Do you perceive yourself as sexually attractive to women?"

"It doesn't matter what I think, since they don't respond to me!" he answered.

My thought was, "Well, that's not really accurate, since it's your dream." As Jung once said about dreaming, "The dreamer is at once scene, actor, prompter, author, audience, and critic." The dreamer was upset at the women but was missing the soul's effort to call attention to his perception of himself.

I asked, "Did all the women in the dream find you unattractive?"

"The one young lady acted very tenderly toward me," he said.

"So you may not be attractive in terms of conventional machismo, but that is not the same as being gay."

In fact, the dreamer didn't find men sexually desirable so much as he struggled to connect with his own masculinity toward women. His account of waking-life relationships reinforced these conclusions. He had a few long-term friendships with women, including some whom he found very desirable. However, he didn't pursue them because he felt he had nothing to offer them.

Once he began to take inventory of his life, the dreamer realized that he had several attractive attributes. In particular, he was going to medical school in waking life. He had care-giving desires, an articulate disposition, and considerable earning potential—three highly attractive characteristics.

He didn't have to risk losing face; he just had to make friends with his real self instead of trying to be a stereotype of a man he wasn't. Based on this dream, I encouraged him to connect with some of his female friends and ask them to evaluate what they thought he could offer a woman in a long-term romantic relationship.

SEEING DEAD PEOPLE

Although troubling, dreams involving people who are dead or who die in the course of the narrative are quite common. (This is different from the dream scenario in which people are actually dead and return to life.) Here, the focus is on people who are already dead when you find them, have died of natural causes (illness, old age, and so on), or are victims of dream violence (perpetrated by either the dreamer or some other person).

In waking life, death causes you to lose access to a person. If someone is dead, you can't really talk to or experience relationships with that person anymore. Or perhaps better, he can no longer speak to you.

In dreams, death is often a means to understanding or resolving your attachment and relationship to either a part of yourself or to another person. To interpret dreams in which some aspect of death is a component, these basic principles can help.

If you (or another dreamer) discover a dead body, look for:

- *A body of the same gender as you, but either younger or older.* This often points to a facet of your identity that you want to reject in waking life (such as being a child).

- *A body of opposite gender.* This image may point to a relationship difficulty with someone of that gender.

- *A body of the same age and gender as you, but with a remarkable feature* (fat, pretty, thin, expensively clothed, decomposed). This often reflects a facet of your life that's in disarray or seems unattainable.

- *Is the discovery the important event, and the body's identifying features irrelevant?* In this case, focus on how you and others in the dream react to the discovery, what you do with the body, and so on.

If you observe someone (known or a stranger) dying of natural causes, consider the following:

- How do you perceive the health (emotional and physical) of authority figures in your life?

- Is the person taking some unhealthy risks in waking life (substance abuse, risky financial decisions, or promiscuity, for example) and denying the possible consequences?

- How close is your relationship with the dying person, and how will the death affect you in waking life?

- Which character attributes (good and bad) does the dying person have, and how do they compare with yours?

If you or someone in the dream acts violently and causes someone's death in a dream, think about the following:

- Is there unspoken resentment concerning the amount of control, irresponsibility, anger, or time this person projects into your life?

- Is the person someone who is out of place in the hierarchy of relationships? For example, if a spouse feels that in-laws interfere with the family excessively, he may dream of them as victims of a crime. Or (as cited in an earlier dream story), if your parents, children, or employers are leaning on you too much, your soul wisdom may "kill" them to show you that you need to push back a bit and rebalance your relationships with those people.

- Does the victim have a personality trait similar to one you dislike in yourself or one you wish you had but don't? Such dreams reflect how you use denial as a defense mechanism. You are either downplaying or denying what you need.

Even though dreams of dead people tend to stay with you because the imagery is so graphic, few people who have them are on the verge of becoming killers.

CHAPTER 23

Self-Illumination Dreams

The dream is the truth. Then they act and do things accordingly.
—Zora Neale Hurston

In terms of transformation, one of the best dreams you can have is one that clarifies your current disposition and mission in life. When this facet of your life seems disordered, dreams can give you clues and cues to help you work away from the false self that's acting as your coping mechanism and toward a real self that optimizes your gifts and abilities.

To reach your destination, it's crucial to find your "real" self. Each of us adopts a personal style of relating that helps us cope with the world around us. To the extent that the world is supportive or threatening, we adopt personality styles that reflect the coping skills we need to survive. This list includes perfectionist traits, seeing yourself as a victim, aggressive tendencies, avoiding intimacy, and many other such maladies.

Dream wisdom is particularly well suited to spurring life development. Since the voice of dreams can have such visceral representations, it often motivates powerful, emotive transactions. Dreams seldom suggest gently shifting your perspective toward a more assertive disposition. Instead, they may portray you as fighting a battle with a legion of persecutors and emerging unscathed!

Universal Dreams

Interestingly, certain dreams appear to be universal across all cultures and ages. Although the contextual elements change from culture to culture depending on the trigger events, it seems that two dream experiences occur among all people: losing teeth and being inappropriately dressed in public.

Dream Stories: Losing Teeth

A military enlisted man reported dreaming:

I am in the mess trying to eat lunch, and my teeth keep coming out.

A career woman in her fifties similarly reported:

I am at a power lunch but am unable to function because my teeth keep slipping out of my mouth.

An 11-year-old girl who recently began menstruating reported:

I am walking home from school, and as I speak with my friends, my teeth keep dropping out of my mouth.

A brilliant young adult contemplating a shift in sexual orientation recounted:

I am standing in front of my bathroom mirror. Four of my teeth, the front two on top and bottom, fall out. I call my brother in so he can observe my predicament.

A college coed recalled this dream:

I am in the bedroom combing my hair. A guy comes in and asks me if I'm in a relationship. I say no. Then he asks me out on a date. I say yes.

He is about to kiss me when I ask him to hold that thought while I go freshen up a bit. I brush my teeth. When I wipe my mouth, my teeth begin falling out! Each one I touch falls out. No bleeding, just empty spaces. I go back in the bedroom, but the guy doesn't seem to notice. Meanwhile, I'm a wreck.

Dream Meaning

In each of these cases, the common trigger event was a move from one position in life to another. The two adults with this dream had an opportunity to move forward in their careers, but they weren't fully confident that they had the skills to function at a higher capacity. The young girl was also assuming a new position in life as she matured from child to young woman. The young man was examining his sense of identity and testing the consequences of his choices. The coed was ambivalent about her relationships and unsure what she wanted.

In each case, the basic interpretation is the same. The dreamer's life is moving in ways the inner self finds intimidating. The dreams represent this ambivalence by reflecting the fear of "losing face."

DREAM COACHING

The question to ask in each instance was the same: "What skills do you think you lack now that you're moving to this new place in your life?" Although the answers were as unique as the dreamers themselves, the dream had the same interpretation in each instance.

This was the right question to ask because it focused on the dreamer as a person rather than the event in the dream itself. When an adult has this dream, it's relatively easy to ask forthrightly what skills may be lacking in regard to a new position in life. When a child has this dream, it may be difficult to determine the specific issue, due to a lack of insight. Nevertheless, helping the dreamer process what new skills must be learned in work or life will help determine the developmental task of the dream.

In the first dream, the dreamer was changing rank from enlisted man to noncommissioned officer. His new position would require working with senior officers, a new experience in his career. He was concerned about the examinations and interaction that would accompany the change.

The second dreamer was an insurance professional who had relocated. While her expertise and experience were unquestionable, she had to reapply for her license, go through reexamination, and so on. This was a new experience after 20-plus years, and not one with which she was comfortable.

The third dreamer was worried about handling the spontaneity of menstruation when she was at school. Keenly aware of the potential for embarrassment, she didn't know how she would respond to the cues from her body. Her mother played an important role in reassuring her that she could handle this new responsibility.

The fourth dreamer wasn't sure that a shift in sexual orientation was really part of "him." He felt pressure from a suitor to consider a liaison. However, there were faith and family issues surrounding his potential decision that posed a possibility for rejection or shame.

The young coed in the last dream was embarrassed about ending a relationship. She would have liked to renew it but feared the opinion of others if she did. When she denied having a significant other, her teeth started falling out. This seemed to indicate embarrassment about not having a relationship or fearing embarrassment in a subsequent one. As in all dreams of losing teeth, the dreamer is afraid of losing face, in this case with her peers.

When such dreams occur, the key is to scan your waking horizons as you evaluate whether you're prepared for a prospective life change. Consider the following:

- If the change is volitional, or an act of will, the dream is examining whether you're fully prepared to accept its implications. Many times, such dreams can reveal blind spots concerning your preparation, or lack thereof, for the next step in your evolution as a person.
- If the change is unavoidable, such as physical maturation, the dream is cuing you to find mentors to guide you.

CHAPTER 24

Relationship Dreams

"In bed my real love has always been the sleep that rescued me by allowing me to dream."

—Luigi Pirandello, Italian author

Genuine intimacy in a relationship or marriage is the thing that separates a good one from a great one. For example, if your marriage is going to go the distance, authentic intimacy will need to supersede the infatuation of newlywed lust.

The challenge is that intimacy is frightening. Letting your whole self be loved includes exposing parts of you that you may not feel good about.

The great news is that your soul hungers for this kind of deep, risky intimacy. If you allow yourself to listen to them, dreams can be a way to prompt you toward greater closeness.

Dream Story: Relationship Fears

An engaged man in his early thirties reported dreaming:

My fiancée and I were on holiday in the first place we went together, but it wasn't the same. We were on the beach, and bombs started to drop from the sky. We ran to the car, but in the panic we got split up. During this time, I was hit by a bomb and my penis was severed! When we met up, later I felt that we had to split up because I was no use to her anymore, and I could never give her kids!

Dream Meaning

When a relationship with someone to whom you are very close goes through transitions, one of the biggest problems you may experience is how to keep the quality of the relationship that attracted you in the first place. This sounds counterintuitive, but even a good transition, such as moving from dating to the permanence of a life partnership, can create stress based on your past experience of marriage (your own or your parents'). The dreamer and his intended were dealing with a new set of relationship issues that involved the anxiety of life commitment.

When a relationship takes on permanence, you may need to grieve not only the past but also the future. Men often grieve the loss of future dating opportunities. It's a strange kind of grief that seems to have roots in ancient times, when men took wives and concubines as status symbols. Now that our culture is monogamous, accepting the loss of other potential lovers is part of the premarital process for some men. Taking a particular woman "emasculates" him with other potential partners.

The dreamer stated that his fiancée was unwilling or unable to respond to him and said, "We haven't been getting along recently, and I'm worried."

DREAM COACHING

Intuitively, I asked, "Your parents' marriage didn't work, did it?"

"No," he said. "It was pretty much a disaster. I don't know which was more pitiful, my efforts to survive childhood or watching my father trying to survive his own adulthood."

The man's grieving over the future had a particular representation in this dream. In particular, I felt he was very anxious about marriage, either because his parents' union failed or because he saw his father act out as a result of feeling inadequate. The dreamer was concerned about repeating the past that he had spent most of his adolescence and adulthood trying to avoid.

There were three growth areas for the dreamer and his fiancée to work on in their relationship. The soul expressed its desire for a healthy marriage through the dream. By moving toward these growth goals, the relationship could handle the transition to permanence with strength and optimism.

- First, the couple had to build their confidence that they would function as a competent team as husband and wife. To do this, they needed to communicate regularly and honestly about what would keep them attractive to each other. They could draw connections with traits they already saw in each other and address how they would like to see those traits grow.

- Second, they needed to ask specific questions about the marriage of the man's parents and their own impending marriage. This way, they would learn what he was trying to avoid in his parents' example. We often repeat what we say we want to avoid because we are so afraid of it that we don't address it honestly.

- Finally, the dream wanted them to be honest with each other about growth areas in their relationship—not in a judgmental way, but in an I-know-we'll-get-better-in-this-area way. Many times, people get married hoping things will change, but they never discuss the growth needs in the relationship. As a consequence, they speak and act as if everything is fine while secretly hoping it won't stay that way.

The dream narrative indicated this by how the man represented himself as unworthy to the woman. Once his situation (his severed member) was revealed, the woman no longer connected with him as a person. One of the hardest parts of marriage is allowing someone else to love the parts of us that we don't necessarily like in ourselves. He was possibly wondering if his fiancée could love the facets of his life or personality that he struggled with himself.

DREAM SYMBOLS

Anna Freud (Sigmund's daughter) said, "Sometimes a cigar is just a cigar." Everyone who looks at the mindscape of dreams to gain insight for living needs to heed her warning.

On the other hand, Freud's Interpretation of Dreams listed more than 90 objects as possible phallic symbols in dreams. This was due to his sexual theory of personality development.

Dream Story: The Snake in the Toilet

In a subsequent dream, the same man reported:

> *I am on a fast-moving train. I know my beloved is on the train somewhere, but I can't find her. As I search, I lift the lid on a toilet and a snake jumps out. I try to subdue it but can't. The scene shifts to us getting a divorce. We have surgery to get microchips removed from our heads so we can be apart.*

Dream Meaning

When someone feels unlovable, he may project all kinds of disasters into his future. Dreaming of getting divorced during their courtship troubled both the dreamer and his significant other. She feared that the dream was prophetic and contemplated ending the engagement.

In reality, the dream was developmental. He needed to see himself as lovable. Reaching a place where he felt okay with himself was crucial to the resolution of the dream and the relationship.

The intervening experience of the snake in the toilet gave some clue to the possible origin of the unlovable feelings. When a father doesn't help a son experience healthy sexual maturity, sexuality becomes a surprising and powerful group of emotions whose influence can be startling.

DREAM COACHING

The question arose: "Your father didn't help you toward manhood, and your mother didn't approve of your maturing, did she?"

"I'm not sure what the right way to be a man is," the man answered.

If a young man's sexuality is exposed at an early age or in unplanned ways, shame becomes part of the mixture. In this instance, the lack of supportive connection with his father, combined with watching his mother experience the pain of a dysfunctional marriage, combined to undermine his identity as a lovable man.

Having the microchips removed was a clue to understanding the soul's call for growth. To experience connection with his beloved, the man had to address the unseen yet ever present influence of another woman in his life. Much of his mother's influence consisted not of overt physical presence but of residual emotional effects. Getting that "microchip" out of the way was the key to the long-term success of that (or any) marriage.

During the engagement, the man's troubling dreams didn't stop completely. However, once the couple began to perceive the dreams as a developmental process rather than a threat to the security of the relationship, the dreams became a means of growing closer to each other.

Dream Story: The Self-Driving Van

A married man in his late thirties reported:

> *I am traveling with my wife in an unfamiliar city. We have a van equipped with a voice-activated phone and map.* [This corresponds to his waking life.] *My wife is standing next to the van, and I am a distance away. I yell to her that I'm bringing the suitcases and it is time to go to the airport. The doors on the van all close automatically, and it drives off as if it has a mind of its own. We expend considerable effort looking for the van, since it "knows" the way to the airport and we don't, due to being in an unfamiliar city. We often spot it along the road but never capture it. I wake up.*

Dream Meaning

The context of the dream was the unfamiliar city. When asked to draw waking parallels, the dreamer reported that the city had an Old World European look to it. The dreamer did in fact have a European vacation planned, and this was a trigger event for the dream.

The experience of the self-driving van and the subsequent pursuit formed the bulk of the dream narrative. Glimpses of the van appearing in the midst of the pursuit were both rewarding and troubling to the dreamer. "It's like the van is toying with me, not evading for its own sake, but staying close enough to tease and far enough away to remain free," he said.

DREAM COACHING

"Who drives the van most," I asked, "you or your wife?"

"It's her car," he stated.

I followed up with, "And how is your marriage these days?"

In fact, the couple was in a season of renewal; both were connecting at deeper levels and being frustrated simultaneously. The man acutely felt both the rewards and frustration of this experience. He was eager for his marriage to grow and take on the characteristics he valued in the relationship. However, he often wanted to push his wife toward his agenda.

"Can you control how another person feels?" I asked.

He realized he couldn't and admitted as much. His enthusiasm for the relationship sometimes resulted in his trying to control how his wife felt instead of experiencing who she was as a person. To pursue someone is a loving gesture of courtship; to try to capture someone is a metaphor for control and pathology.

Dreams can also chart the evolution of our capacity for intimacy, as this dream shows:

Dream Story: Killing the Queen of the Castle

A young man reported dreaming:

> I am in a castle with my girlfriend. I am rescuing her. Dressed in the stereotypical "Prince Valiant" attire, I move gracefully through the obstacles and creatures that thwart my efforts. However, the queen of

the castle confronts me, and I must behead her to be liberated. I do so,
but I immediately experience some regret at having completed that task.
We leave.

Dream Meaning

In this dream, the dreamer feels both victorious and burdened by the content
of the narrative. The obstacles were all impersonal until he faced the queen of the
castle. At that point, he seems ambivalent about the course of his actions. The
mission of the dream was to leave, but the means of doing so were troublesome.

DREAM COACHING

The question in my mind was, "Why was killing the queen of the castle, who
had orchestrated the various obstacles, any more troubling than negotiating
the obstacles themselves?" The dreamer had a connection to the queen somehow. I asked who the most influential woman in his life was.

"My girlfriend, definitely," he answered.

"And if I had asked you that question six months ago?"

"My mother."

Of course, the dream wasn't coaching the young man to behead his own
mother! However, it was illuminating an emerging growth cycle in his life. In
order to fulfill the need for connection, romance, and relationship to a woman
who could conceivably become his wife, he needed to leave the "queen," no
matter what the cost.

After a growth dream, you wake with a feeling of motivation to act upon
your life and move it in a new direction. For this young man, the dream task
of slaying the queen of the castle represented the life task of placing a new person at the center of his influence and attention. After 20-plus years of living
with his parental family at the center of his world, he saw, through the dream,
that some pain and regret would naturally accompany that task.

SEX AND DREAMS

Sex frequently shows up in dreams. William Domhoff, in his book *Finding the Meaning of Dreams*, reports that 93 percent of men and 68 percent of women report having dreams of being engaged in sexual behavior. Yet women report observing sexual behavior almost five times more than men (32 percent versus 7 percent).

In dreams, sex often has a lot more to do with the dreamer's desire to connect with people than with wanting to participate in particular physical acts. Much of this relates to the fact that our culture treats sex and intimacy as synonymous, although they certainly don't automatically equate with each other. In playful or wish-fulfillment dreams, sex is typically pleasant. When the dream of a sexual experience is very troubling, however, any one of the following scenarios can point to a reason.

- *You are having sex with an inappropriate person:* a subordinate, a much older person, a much younger person, a married person, or someone other than your spouse or significant other.

- *You are having sex in an inappropriate place.*

- *The sex is particularly graphic* or somewhat "kinky" in comparison with your waking life preferences.

- *Your sexual partner is contrary to your actual sexual orientation.*

There are six common categories of sex dreams. In dreams, where and why you have sex are both important to the interpretation, as follows:

- *Sex on a beach (in the mountains, in a meadow, and so on) with a known person.* This dream is usually a garden-variety wish-fulfillment dream.

- *Consensual sex with a stranger of either gender.* Many times, the other party in your liaison personifies a personality attribute. Such dreams often call you to look at the strengths or weaknesses of your nocturnal partner to see areas of your life in which you are either over- or underfunctioning.

- *Consensual sex with a known, inappropriate person* (a subordinate, a married person, a student). Two dominant themes emerge. First, the person may be someone who has a character attribute that you admire or for whom you feel genuine affection. In other words, you really like the person in waking life, but not *that* way. This could be a warning, however, to keep your mind clear about what's appropriate with this person in the real world.

Second, the inappropriate liaison may indicate deprivation or denial of your sexual identity. The most inappropriate of liaisons, such as relationships condemned by social authority, can create strong emotions in the dreamer. A taboo sexual liaison in a dream often points to a traumatic past or a potentially traumatic future unless the dreamer gets some outside help to cope with the stress of sexual relations.

- *Violent sex with a known person.* This scenario could indicate unhealthy control issues or toxic intimacy that prevent you from being yourself with the other person or participating fully in other relationships.

- *Violent/ violating sex or sexual contact with an unknown person.* Such dreams can reflect persecution or shame. An earlier dream story involved a young man being touched by an alien—a reflection of the shame he felt about his sexuality.

- *Violent sex that you instigate.* Dreams with this theme can reflect anger or lack of resolution about your sexuality. We punish those parts of ourselves

171

that we judge harshly. Over time, this approach festers into feelings of disconnection that the soul wants to resolve, but the filter of personality restrains our perception.

In sum, sexuality is a very mysterious, powerful influence in our lives. It has emotional and spiritual dimensions that reflect our innermost passions. Because sex is so close to our strongest emotions, it frequently becomes a dream symbol. Further, since the sexual experience can be very exciting or traumatic, it's easily connected with similar aspects of our lives.

Relationship-Evaluation Dreams

There's nothing so sweet in life as love's young dream.
—Thomas Moore

Often, you can evaluate a decision prior to actually making it through a dream experience. If you reflect on your life, you may think to yourself, "If only I had known it would be like this." Through disciplined dream collection and interpretation, you have the opportunity to know what it would be like.

Dream Story: Gasping Fish-Children

Geoff, a man in his mid-thirties, reported this dream:

I have gone fishing. Each fish I catch has a head that reminds me somewhat of the face of one of my children. Suddenly, the fish heads all transform into exact representations of my children's faces. I am greatly troubled when I notice them gasping for air, in the manner of fish out of water.

Dream Meaning

The basic elements of context, experience, and ending were all prominent in this narrative. The context was fishing, since that was the only setting described in the narrative. The dream reported only the act of fishing, without elaboration. The experiences were catching fish, noticing their appearance, watching their transformation, and feeling regret for their circumstances. The ending is the fish-children, gasping for air.

The context of fishing was very important. In fact, Geoff was "fishing around" for a new relationship that would possibly replace the one that had produced the children in the dream. In doing so, he was focused on the ache he felt about an unfulfilling situation instead of the consequences his action would have for others.

The experiences of the dream gave him a chance to evaluate the impact of his "fishing around" on his children. The secondary elaboration of the narrative was that the fish heads went through a transformation process that concluded with an exact representation of his children's faces at their current, waking-life ages.

The experience of regret over their gasping was pivotal because it called Geoff to recognize the consequences of taking the children out of their familiar environment. The dream showed the children experiencing frightening, life-threatening fear. This became the life application interpretation of the dream.

DREAM COACHING

In waking life, Geoff had minimized the effects a divorce would have on his children. When confronted with the decision-making process about a possible divorce and its impact, he articulated several profound consequences of divorce upon children. The dream broke through his denial structure with the reality that actions have consequences.

This dream was very difficult for him to experience because he was contemplating divorce in the context of his own desires. It confronted him with the truth that his own desires were not the only ones that merited consideration.

If he pursued his chosen course of action, he would deprive the fish-children of their resources for life.

How could Geoff's waking self grow from this dream? If the soul has an appetite for well-being and fulfillment, could staying in an unfulfilling marriage work toward his goal of wellness? He spent several weeks reflecting on the dream.

The fishing context was the key. Fishing is a proactive exercise in catching something that doesn't just walk up and surrender to you. We fish for clues, fish for food in the fridge, or troll around the Internet for information.

Perhaps Geoff needed to fish for his wife instead of abandoning his family. If he could connect with her, he wouldn't have to pull his children out of water and change their environment in such drastic ways. It was a challenging idea for him to embrace.

When Geoff began "courting" his wife and actively pursuing her again, the relationship experienced wonderful new vitality that greatly increased his satisfaction with the marriage. He faced some relationship laziness in his life that had resulted in trying to solve the legitimate problem (an unfulfilling relationship) the wrong way. True intimacy is something that takes proactive searching, just like fishing.

Real Life Offers Clues

In dreams such as this, the real-life context is crucial to determining the dream's growth message. Without knowing the dreamer's waking reality, accurate interpretation would be next to impossible. The knowledge that Geoff was unhappy in his marriage provided cues for the growth structure the dream was trying to point out.

Dream wisdom has an excellent way of leading you toward waking-life truths you may prefer to ignore or deny. Geoff rightly discerned that "fishing" could create a doorway to a more fulfilling relationship than his current one. For the fishing to work, however, it had to be done correctly. Fishing in the "wrong pond" or catching the "wrong fish" was only going to create more pain, not resolve the pain he was experiencing.

In waking life, Geoff had avoided fishing in the "right pond," which was detrimental to his personal goals rather than furthering them. How often have you wanted the right thing but gone about it the wrong way, thus moving you farther from your objective? Because dreams can show us truth that's unadulterated by our own denial, the good ones "grow us up" rather than indulge our immaturity.

CHAPTER 26

Work-Related Dreams

The only credential asked of them was the boldness to dream.

—Moss Hart

Dream Story: Help Staying on Task

An executive in his early forties reported dreaming:

I have rented a U-Haul truck and need to return it. A coworker volunteers to help. The scene changes, and now I'm in the rental office trying to administer the process while he waits in the passenger seat of my car. Everything goes wrong. Just as I'm giving up, he intervenes and rescues the process, getting me back on task.

Dream Meaning

The context for the dream was the dreamer's car and the rental office where everything went awry. The context offers two important symbols, as driving a car often symbolizes being in control, regardless of whether the dreamer actually is. In the other context, the rental office, the dreamer's skills and resources were at the mercy of another person. The dream ends not with his successful completion of the task but with his simply surrendering control to the coworker.

DREAM COACHING

This executive had recently been promoted and was developing his "personal firewall" of associates. Being new, he was still covering for his weaknesses, but he knew he needed to build a team to protect himself and his agency from those weaknesses. Selecting people to bring into his inner circle was a matter of significant concern. The dream guided him to choose the dream companion as part of his "firewall."

It also persuaded the dreamer to live with, rather than deny, his tendency to lose track of details. Although he initially feared building his support team, he knew it was imperative if he was going to be effective in his position.

Dream Story: A Revelatory Snake

In the following dream, the image of a snake presented a solution to a scientific problem. In 1890, German chemist F.A. Keule was trying to understand atoms and their work in the structure of benzene compounds. He reported the following dream:

> *The atoms were juggling before my mind's eye . . . [I] could now distinguish larger structures of different forms, moving in a snakelike and twisted way. Suddenly…one of the snakes got hold of its own tail and the whole structure was mockingly twisting before my own eyes. I awoke…*

When Keule woke up, he saw very clearly in his mind's eye the circlelike structure of the benzene molecule. He concluded, "Let us learn to dream, gentlemen, and then perhaps we may find the truth."

The reality is that dreams depend more on the dreamer than on the symbols. Always turn to your life, not symbol dictionaries, as your first resource for determining what a particular symbol may mean in a specific dream.

CHAPTER 27

Violent Dreams

Those who have compared our life to a dream were right...
we sleeping wake and waking sleep.

—Montainge

W hen there is a violent element in the dream, it usually indicates strong feelings are at play. Often, the dreamer is not willing to face those feelings—or the issues that are giving rise to those feelings—in her day-to-day life.

Dream Story: Paying with Her Life

A woman in her early forties reported dreaming:

I am at a gas station with my friends. Nobody has money for gas, so I go in to pay. While I'm in there, an armed robbery begins. I walk out and get shot in the back as I go to my car. No one seems to notice me.

Dream Meaning

This dream had a clarifying role in the dreamer's waking life as she tried to experience healthy connections with people. In waking life, she was moving from distance and isolation toward a healthier shared experience in friendship.

However, the feelings were unfamiliar and therefore difficult.

The context was the gas station, a place that refuels vehicles and sells provision for modern life. For the most part, gas stations are unavoidable for most people and provide refreshment as well as gas and other automotive products. The dreamer was a frequent "pit-stop" person.

The experiences of the dream were numerous and implied as well as literal to the dream narrative. The implied experiences included buying gas, taking inventory of who has money, encountering the robbers, exiting the building, being shot, and being neglected.

The ending of the dream seemed to be the neglect of the dreamer's need for help. Although her need is profound, no one reacts to it. No other resolution is indicated.

DREAM COACHING

I asked, "Do you ever feel that you're the only 'responsible one' in your life?"

"Sometimes I get so tired of doing a thousand little things my drinking friends can't do for themselves," she replied.

The dream provoked anger as the dreamer realized that she was providing for her friends yet again. Wherever they were going, she intuitively called it a shared journey that everyone wanted to take, but only she had the resources to transport the group. Her car and her money for gas indicated this.

The robbery was not simply a dream event but a metaphor for her life. She felt as though she was being "robbed" time and again by a group of people who neglected their individual responsibilities in favor of her direction and providence. The result was that she often felt depleted.

Being ignored was the growth aspect of the dream, however. I asked if the dreamer called for help, and she couldn't recall doing so. Often, when people experience a high level of caregiving in relationships, it's a way to mask their own needs for support or connection. By being the "strong one," the dreamer had been able to keep others at arm's length.

It was a challenge for the woman to realize that asking for help or acknowledging her own appropriate need for connection and dependence on others was part of what would bring healing to her friendships. Once she allowed herself to have and express needs that others could identify with, perhaps she would experience mutual friendship instead of entangling dependencies.

The timing of the dream played an important role in the interpretation. The woman had the dream after an extended period of sobriety, but many among her circle of friends still had alcohol issues. The dreamer wasn't part of a recovery group but was doing it "on her own." Her motivation was admirable, but the lack of support created an environment in which her drinking friends depleted her financial and emotional resources.

CHAPTER 28

Protection Dreams

Mankind is a dream of a shadow. But when a God-given brightness
comes, a radiant light rests on men, and a gentle life.

—Pindar, c. 518-438 B.C.

I t's said that those who fail to learn from the past are destined to relive it.
Toward this end, dreams can be relentless guardians of the soul, casting
warnings about every relationship you experience. The warnings are not
necessarily prophetic, but they are reminders to stand up for yourself. Once
you experience a relationship that goes badly, it's important not to put yourself
in other situations where you're vulnerable.

This is true of both romantic and workplace relationships. In both career
and dating, the demands of others can be controlling and leave you wondering what happened to you and your aspirations.

Dream Story: A Hint of Sacrifice

A married mother with one child reported dreaming:

I have been at church at Christmastime with my daughter, but it's not
kid-friendly and offers few craft activities for her, so I leave feeling disap-
pointed. When I get out to my car, a driver (whom she didn't know or
employ in waking life) *is there to take us home. However, he seems*

suspicious to me. As we travel, I realize he isn't taking us home but to another place that reminds me of my childhood home. I'm getting ready to hit him with my purse and make a run for it with my daughter when he hits me first. I wake up.

The context of Christmas combined with the experience of feeling disappointed for her child was the main interpretive clue for the dream. Her child was getting the short end of the deal, even at church.

When an unknown man took control of their progress by driving them, but not toward home, my sense was that an authority figure from outside the home was controlling the family environment. This left the options of the woman's father and father-in-law, both of whom were still alive, or an employer. Neither father had day-to-day influence on the dreamer's life, but work certainly did.

DREAM COACHING

I inquired, "Do you feel that the demands of others are undermining your care of your daughter?"

"It does seem like she's getting less of me than I really want to give her," she replied.

I asked who or what was contributing to that situation, and we examined not only the demands of her part-time job but also her husband's required overtime. These factors were conspiring to leave the family feeling strung out and emotionally drained.

Omens from the Past

Another variation on "protection" dream narratives occurs when a dream compares a bad or abusive waking-life experience from the past to a new or yet undefined experience.

Dream Story: A Warning?

Therese, a 21-year-old single woman, reported dreaming:

> *It's around Christmastime. My dad is in the kitchen helping mom cook dinner, and my new boyfriend and I are sitting on the couch watching TV. My mom asks me to go to the store with her, and I agree. I tell my boyfriend I'll be back in 10 minutes. When we return, he's left a note saying that he was sick of waiting and left. All of a sudden, I'm in my nightclothes and telling Mom that I'm going to take a bath. I walk to the bathroom and see the closed shower curtain and the soft glow of candles.*
>
> *I pull back the shower curtain and scream when I see the bathtub full of blood, my dog's head nailed to the wall, and "666, F*#$ you, stupid bitch. I never want to see you again." written in blood on the wall. Then I hear a recording of my boyfriend's voice saying "F*#$ you" over and over again coming from a rotating miniature Christmas tree on the counter. I pick up little origami ducks on a small table. They explode, and blood splashes on my face and gets in my hair. I wake up crying.*

Dream Meaning

Dreams aren't good at differentiating experience, which is one of the troubling things about them. This dream projected the experience of a prior painful, long-term relationship onto the potential new relationship. The new boyfriend was cast as a "bad boyfriend" to the nth degree. Why? There is something worse than not having a boyfriend, and that's having the wrong one. The dream let Therese know that she was fine regardless of whether she was connected to a boy or independent, but the prior bad relationship went on longer than it should have.

DREAM COACHING

Therese pleaded, "I hope someone can help me with this; it's really been messing with me. The boyfriend I have now treats me like a princess, and I'm very happy with him."

I asked, "Things got pretty rough in your first serious relationship, didn't they?"

She replied, "I've been out of a bad four-year relationship for about eight months, and I'm now dating someone new."

"That prior relationship did get pretty bad at times, didn't it?"

"It was awful. I did a lot of things just to keep him happy, even though I was feeling pretty bad about myself and him."

I questioned whether the first boyfriend trashed some of her religious convictions, if sex was a way of placating him, and whether he was jealous of her closeness to her family—a closeness he didn't necessarily experience with his own family or perceive as valuable. I also inquired whether her first sexual experience occurred in this relationship, and in a way that wasn't planned.

"Does any of this fit?" I said.

"All of it fits," she replied.

I counseled Therese that probably the worst thing about that relationship was that in trying to keep her boyfriend happy, she felt she had lost what was important to her. The growth issue was to stick up for herself as she moved into intimacy within this new relationship. Her dream was ready to teach her how, and its message was apparent.

The soul wanted to protect what was important to the dreamer. The dream was reminding her, "Don't lose what's important to you; keep it out front in the new relationship." For example, if the new boyfriend couldn't handle her religious convictions, family relationships, and so on, she wasn't obligated to continue the relationship, hoping to "work around" their differences.

The dream was a warning to avoid relationships that isolated her from others. Healthy relationships feature a normal amount of sharing with others who are important to you. Again, this dream was a call to defend the relationships and issues that Therese felt were important. Her dream wisdom was warning her not to surrender to demands of the new boyfriend at the expense of her family relationship. She could connect with her new boyfriend in healthy ways when the two of them had the time, but she could also connect with her family as needed. Moreover, if the boyfriend was interested in a healthy relationship, he would welcome the opportunity to know her family as well.

If the new boyfriend had concerns that the two of them couldn't "do what they wanted" when her family was around, that would create harmful isolation. The dream was sounding a clarion call to Therese to avoid being dominated as she was in her first relationship. She should be able to express her connections with her boyfriend privately and be publicly connected with her family in happy, balanced ways.

"How does your new boyfriend treat you, honestly?" I asked.

"He treats me like a princess," she replied.

I counseled her that if he ever chose to treat her any differently, she should run, not walk, toward the nearest exit. Her soul had given her the gift of seeing that life is more than a boyfriend; it's your family, other loved ones, and values, and you are entitled to all of them.

A note for dads. This dream carries an interesting message for fathers. (Because I have three daughters, I notice these things.) When my daughters start dating, my wife and I need to be proactive in assessing and coaching them in loving, connected ways. In the dream, dad is there and "not there" as he provides food for Therese without otherwise participating in the dream narrative. I think the father-daughter relationship is a crucial one that daughters need when they start dating.

CHAPTER 29

Grief Dreams

Thrice I would have thrown my arms about her neck, and thrice the ghost embraced fled from my grasp; like a fluttering breeze, like a fleeting dream.

—Virgil

The death of a loved one causes profound grief, but life also presents many other experiences for which grief is the appropriate response, including:

- A lost relationship
- A period of life that was idyllic
- An opportunity
- An image of yourself that you realize is unrealistic
- The loss of physical health, or other experiences that dramatically or traumatically thrust change upon you.

Grieving a Relationship

It's common to experience several love relationships prior to settling on a life partner, and the relationships we go through as part of learning how love works often lead to grief.

A dream in which you are dead but interact with the living world is often a "living with grief" dream. Likewise, when you experience people who have died as being alive in your dreams, your soul is often calling you to grieve incomplete aspects of your relationship with those people in waking life.

Dream Story: An Ex-Lover Dreams of His Own Funeral

A single woman in her early twenties reported the following dream that her ex-boyfriend conveyed to her:

> *I am at my own funeral, walking around in a ghostlike state, observing others. I see a person who I know is my wife. She is very upset. I look to see who I married. I catch a glimpse of her face, and it's my ex-girlfriend, who I broke up with eight months ago.*

Dream Meaning

The ex-boyfriend reported the dream to the woman, and she brought it to me for interpretation. She was concerned that perhaps the dream was prophetic and she should try to work things out with her ex, who had initiated the breakup. It had been a three-year relationship that began when she was 17 and he was 20. After eight months apart at the time of the dream, he had started a new monogamous long-term relationship.

The dream's context was the dreamer being present at his own funeral. This context was important because of the perspective it allowed. Obviously, the soul is representing some form of what could have been or what is.

His experience of touring around the room was a way of evaluating his life. Socrates said, "Know thyself." One of the best ways to know yourself is to examine your life decisions and see how they're working out for you and others. Thinking about how people will remember you after you die is a great way to evaluate your actions while you are alive.

The experience of observing his grieving wife held interest on several levels. First, he could see whom he married. Second, by gauging her grief, he could get a sense of the quality of their relationship.

Seeing his ex-girlfriend as his wife in the dream, instead of his present girlfriend or an unrecognizable female stranger, troubled him. It raised the question of whether he had missed his destiny by ending the relationship, and made the dream stick with him more than if he had dreamed of his present romantic interest or a stranger.

When the grieving widow raised her face to look at him, the dream ended abruptly. There was no connection or spiritual reuniting. This ending shed the most interpretive light on the situation.

The dream ended with the finality of separateness. The dreamer died and experienced the world he knew in a disconnected way. The ex-girlfriend (seen as his wife) attended the funeral to grieve, with no indication of trying to get to her deceased "husband." When he saw her, he didn't connect with her but remained separate in death at the dream's conclusion.

DREAM COACHING

Since the dream was really his and not hers, the interpretation focused on his grief over dissolving the relationship. Because a dream is a gift of truth from your own soul, even when you dream about someone else, it's a dream about how your soul is building and designing interactions with the other person.

I asked the woman, "Have you recently started dating again? You probably waited longer than he did, but now you are moving on, and he knows it, right?"

The answer to both questions was affirmative.

For the dreamer, the message was to realize that he and his former girlfriend were both moving on from their relationship together. It was wisdom that required grieving on his part. His new girlfriend had many admirable qualities, but he missed some of the attributes of his prior girlfriend.

For the ex-girlfriend, the dream narrative was a little destabilizing for her in her new relationships. What if she and the dreamer were destined to be together?

I asked, "Were you more motivated than he was in life and the relationship?"

"I have my associate's degree and real estate license, and I'm working on my bachelor's. He hasn't done much yet," she answered.

The woman was obviously disappointed by the rejection she felt, but at the same time, she realized her aspirations were different from his in many areas of life.

"You spent a fairly substantial amount of your emotional resources helping him feel good about himself, didn't you?" I inquired.

"I felt that I always had to give in to what he wanted or expected out of the relationship," she admitted. If he didn't quite control her, it's fair to consider that his needs put her on the defensive.

Your dreams speak to your own developmental work as a person. This dreamer tried to make his dream his ex-girlfriend's problem, but this is contrary to what dream wisdom is all about.

I would have counseled the young man to evaluate his new and past relationship very carefully. There were probably some things about his first girlfriend that he valued more in their absence than he did in the relationship.

Dream Story: Wounds That Need Healing

When a relationship ends, the regrets of that relationship usually need time to heal before a new relationship can begin in a healthy manner. A single woman in her twenties reported dreaming:

> *I am driving in a storm when a truck hits my car broadside. The injuries are significant, and I go to the hospital for treatment. My boyfriend* [now my ex-boyfriend in waking life] *is there, but seems very disconnected with the gravity of my condition.*

DREAM COACHING

The question arose, "What pain did you experience in the relationship, where the boyfriend pretty much hung you out to dry?"

"I got pregnant and then had a miscarriage," she said. "He never even came to the hospital."

Like many couples, they hadn't planned for her to get pregnant, and her subsequent health problems put unbearable pressure on the relationship. When the demands of maturity became evident, he was nowhere to be found.

The dreamer needed time to grieve her relationship choices, the miscarriage, and the rejection she felt. These are hard tasks, because the waking world says to jump back into life and try for another relationship. That was the last thing she needed to do.

I encouraged her to start by seeing her relationship needs as important and valid before beginning physical intimacy with a man, as well as to seek partners who could accept her terms. By removing himself from the reality of her pregnancy and miscarriage, her former boyfriend proved that he had not really allowed himself to connect with her in waking life.

The relationship choices leading up to the miscarriage were the next level of grief to work through. She hadn't planned for many of the choices that led to such profound consequences for her, including having sex and getting pregnant.

Finally, she had to grieve the rejection she felt when her physical and emotional pain was treated as unimportant. Men often lack the depth of grief that women experience after miscarriage. However, the fact that her boyfriend negated and abandoned those feelings took the typical heartache of a breakup to a much deeper level.

The Effects of Abuse

A relationship in which abuse occurred or was allowed to occur requires a good deal of grieving. When someone abuses you, or you feel that someone else allowed you to be abused, the emotional hurt lasts long after the immediate pain of the event. In addition to grief over the abuse itself, a very toxic mixture of guilt, shame, and anger causes hurt in the soul.

Dreams often have a role to play in exorcising some of that pain. The soul wants to protect itself from the consuming forces of the world as expressed through the unmanaged desires of others. When someone abuses you, it indicates a complete inability to appreciate you as a person. Your soul, however, cares about affirming that you are a person.

Dream Story: Self-Defense

An 18-year-old woman reported this dream:

We're all in the car (stepfather, mom, stepsisters, and me). I say, "I told Mom." My two stepsisters disappear out of the car. My stepdad raises his arm to hit me over the head. I notice my mom just sitting there. I hit him in the arm and wake up.

Dream Meaning

The car was the stepfather's control mechanism in waking life, so in the dream, he was driving—"in charge"—again. This was the context.

The experiences of the stepdad being in charge and the mom sitting there motionless formed the center of the interpretation. In waking life, being caught had ended the abuse, but a number of years went by before that happened. While the trauma was occurring, it seemed to the dreamer as though no one had the power to help her.

In waking life, the abuser had used fear and threats to ensure silence. The dreamer felt she couldn't speak out. However, in the dream, she had the ability to do so, and she did. The soul was defending her (and itself).

After speaking up, the dreamer acted physically to defend herself. Again, this was a scenario that had seemed impossible in waking life. The dream asserted that self-defense was appropriate and empowered her to act on her own behalf.

D R E A M   C O A C H I N G

I asked, "Did he use the car to isolate you?"

"Yeah, he would take me places," she said. "He also talked to me privately in the car and said things that made me sick."

The soul was inviting the young woman to healing and growth. Her stepfather had taken away three important things, and her dream wanted to give them all back.

He had taken away her right to say no. The abuse occurred when she was 15, still young. He had used his position as an adult to take away something that she was entitled to as a person: the right to have authority over her body. In her dream, the soul invited her to reclaim that right by using words to defend herself.

He had damaged her relationship with her mother. The dream invites the dreamer back into that relationship. Needless to say, the mom's marriage to a man who became dangerous to her daughter strained their relationship. Once the mom realized what was going on, she did act to protect her daughter. However, her ignorance of the situation had created a season in life where she did nothing.

He had made her powerless. Finally, the dream invited the dreamer to stand up to her stepfather. Psychologically, she needed to know that she had that power and was entitled to do so. Her stepdad's ability to control her life and behavior was over. In the dream, she struck first, he couldn't hurt her again, and the dream ended. He no longer "drove" her.

This dream was not a magic bullet that immediately and completely healed the effects of the abuse. However, it did open doors for the dreamer to see herself as empowered despite the victimization she had experienced. I'm proud of the young woman who shared this dream with me. She will define her life in terms larger than the insidious designs of evil-minded people who think only of their own desires.

Dreams That Offer Comfort

Grieving is one the most difficult tasks of life. We're responding to the loss of something valuable, but dream growth can help us prepare for and work through the grief process.

In grieving dreams, the dreamer may be working on his own mortality or that of a loved one. Either way, the resulting growth can lead to the soul's comfort and strength for the inevitability of human frailty.

These dreams are troubling at one level because they confront our own denial about death and grief. I recall being at a 70th birthday celebration and hearing the daughter honor her father with these words: "I thank God for my dad, who has always been and always will be with me." The man had been in poor health, and as the words left her mouth, I thought to myself, "Someday you may crash awfully hard, dear."

Dreams provide a strong grief framework because while they are frank (sometimes brutally so), they often point toward the healing place in the dreamer's soul that will help resolve the grief. The key is to not be sidetracked by a dream's frankness. Often, dreamers panic at what they perceive to be prophetic elements of the dream, and neglect to interpret it as a gift from their soul. Instead, death dreams often motivate people to run headlong in the opposite direction. The futility of this should be apparent.

Dream Story: Seeking a Dwelling

A man in his mid-seventies recounted this dream:

> *I am wandering through an unfamiliar place, like an English village, looking for lodging. An upset feeling creeps over me as I begin to think there isn't a place for me. The feeling is similar to that of a lost child. A voice that I perceive to be Christ tells me there is a place for me and guides me to it.* [He never sees the figure in the dream, just "feels" him.] *I find the accommodations very pleasing.*

Dream Meaning

The dreamer viewed this dream as a premonition, since he perceived his age to be "old." His father had died well before that age. Consequently, he was increasingly aware of life as a temporary experience.

The context of the village was compelling. It wasn't a hotel or place of temporary dwelling, but implicit to the dreamer was the reality that he was seeking a long-term residence. He was an avid traveler who enjoyed meeting the "old-timers" in small towns he visited. Consequently, he intuitively knew that it was his job to find a permanent dwelling place in this village.

For the previous 15 years, the dreamer also had struggled somewhat with his sense of connection with faith and the Divine. Numerous life influences caused this struggle to transform into a journey of sorts. In waking life, he confessed a Christian experience that indicated belief in a heavenly afterlife.

This faith was the trigger event for the Christ experience in the dream. The dreamer was contemplating not only the temporary nature of his life but also what came next. The presence of Christ, who had prepared a place for him, provided tremendous reassurance about his existence and connection with the Divine.

DREAM COACHING

The growth result of this dream was a decrease in the dreamer's anxiety in waking life. His connection with the Divine became a part of his life that he shared more transparently with his extended family, to his benefit and theirs. It benefited him in that his dream experience formed the basis for an ongoing confession of faith, as well as reassurance to his family that he understood his connection with the Divine in ways that "prepared" him for the reality of his own mortality.

Dream Story: Seeing a Ghost

In addition to preparing us for our own mortality, sometimes a dream prepares us for the mortality of another. A young woman in her twenties reported:

I don't remember all the particulars of my dream, but I do know that at one point I was walking down the street when I ran into a little girl. I instantly realized that the child was myself at a younger age. I'm 22 now, and the child was about 4 or 5. I knew I was looking at a ghost, but I'm not sure why. I gave her/me a hug, and she told me that everything was going to be okay.

She added, "I'm stretching things here, but I'm hoping that may be some sort of message for me about my father, who's struggling with brain cancer."

Dream Meaning

The dream was troubling to the woman because of seeing herself as a ghost. Her father had been battling cancer for quite a while, and the dream occurred near the end of his last chemotherapy treatments.

That the context was "going somewhere" was indicated by the simplicity of the sidewalk setting. No indication is given as to the weather, the purpose of her travel, or where the sidewalk was located in waking life. Secondary elaboration could have created these choices, but they were unnecessary.

The experiences of the dream were meeting a younger self in ghost form, hugging, and reassurance. This image of a self who meets a displaced self is fairly common, particularly when waking life is moving the dreamer from one identity to another. Given the dreamer's age in waking life, a dream experience like this would have been expected. However, the waking condition of her father made it even more relevant.

The child-self was at the age when most of our parental memories are just forming. Prior to age four or five, specific recall of Mom or Dad as separate from us is not readily accessible. However, after that age, we begin to appreciate our parents as unique people.

The younger self could also have been a condensation figure of Dad, as in "Daddy's little girl." The dreamer readily agreed that death was frequently represented in her dreams, captured in the "ghost girl" of this narrative. Because she was fearful about her father's prognosis, the ghost girl was a safe way to represent the possibility of his death while also confronting it.

DREAM COACHING

The dreamer was coaching herself to prepare for an identity independent of her in waking life. The self she met was a child who could only experience life as dependent on her parents. The self she was now was a person who would, tragically, have to experience life as a product of her father's love but independent of his presence.

Although the dreamer held out hope for prophetic insight concerning her father's well-being, the dream was more related to her own fortitude during her father's struggle. Her dream encouraged her that she needn't let the fear of this cancer define who she was. (If you let it, cancer can direct all the resources of life.)

Her dream also encouraged her that she would be all right. The dreamer had lived her life only in the context of being her father's daughter, but that would change soon, as she necessarily became more independent while he went through treatment.

Resolution of grief is another important facet of dreams and the grieving process. Death is a life transition that can be very painful to manage, and we do well to muster all our resources to work through the process of recovering from our grief.

Dream Story: A Widow Meets Her Husband Just After Death

Many of these dream stories present ways that faith and love work together to help us cope with the reality of death. A forty-something widow recounted this dream, which she had for five nights after her husband died:

> *We were meeting in a room like a hospital.* [She called it that because all the patients, including her husband, were wearing white.] *After a few minutes of talking, he says the visiting time is over, and all the patients walk out the same door together.*

She continued, "Each night, I had the same dream, but my late husband appeared a little more decrepit in his mannerisms and appearance. On the fifth night of the dream, I awakened hoping I won't have the dream anymore since he looked so bad. I never have the dream again."

Dream Meaning

The trigger event was obvious—the death of the dreamer's husband. Suddenly, the nature of life and afterlife, which had been abstract, was an immediate concern for her. Her husband had been chronically ill with kidney disease for quite a while, so although sudden, his death was not completely unexpected. She remembered wondering what happened to him after he died.

The experiences of the conversation and transition from the visiting area to the "unknown place" were important components of the dream interpretation. In waking life, her husband had passed away alone; she had stepped outside his hospital room to attend to personal needs. While she accepted the innocence of her leaving (it wasn't due to apathy), she remembered feeling great regret that he had died alone.

DREAM COACHING

This dream provided resolution and comfort in that the woman was allowed to rehearse the many things that she felt she would have said if she had known that night was to be his last in waking life. While she couldn't recall the details of the five conversations, each ended with the feeling that it was okay for the husband to be in this unknown place in the dream. The dream comforted the widow and her son with the knowledge that their departed loved one had not simply transformed into nonbeing.

Looking back on the dream, the woman viewed it as acceptance of her husband's crossing over. His death while she was absent had burdened her soul with a level of grief that was hard to take in. Consequently, her dreams broke it down into five smaller, more manageable experiences, each demonstrating her husband's need to "leave" the hospital due to increasing deterioration. Finally, when the dream concluded, she found she could be relieved by the end of his suffering rather than consumed with regret over not being with him when he died.

Dream Story: Jung Confronts Mortality

Carl Jung himself had a dream that confronted him with questions of mortality and the afterlife that he had ignored most of his professional life. He reported:

Six weeks after his death, my father appeared to me in a dream. Suddenly, he stood before me and said that he was coming back from his holiday. He had made a good recovery and was now coming home. I thought he would be annoyed with me for having moved into his room. But not a bit! Nevertheless, I felt ashamed because I had imagined he was dead. Two days later, the dream was repeated. My father had recovered and was coming home, and again I reproached myself because I had thought he was dead. Later, I kept asking myself, "What does it mean that my father returns in dreams and that he seems so real?" It was an unforgettable experience, and it forced me for the first time to think about life after death. (From Jung, *Memories, Dreams, and Reflections*, 1963.)

CHAPTER 30

Mortality Dreams

A dream is a scripture, and many scriptures are nothing but dreams.
—Umberto Eco

Dream Story: An Unclear Directive

A married woman in her forties reported dreaming:

> *My cousin* [her best friend in waking life, who had pancreatic cancer that had spread to his liver] *is sick unto death. I am visiting him in his last days, and Christ comes and leads me to a shallow grave, freshly filled. He says, "You can do something about this." I wake up.*

Dream Meaning

The dream troubled the woman because it occurred after her cousin's death. Over time, she started to feel survivor's guilt that she had somehow forgotten to do "something" for him. While she wasn't undone in day-to-day functioning, she felt a gnawing sense of "What if?"

The contexts of the dream were the cousin's hospice room and the cemetery. There is no mode of transportation; the scene simply shifts from A to B as the dreamer turns away from her cousin.

The experiences were seeing her cousin, seeing Christ, seeing the grave, and hearing the words spoken. The dream ended with the directive from Christ. There was no resolution about what should be done or when. This was disquieting for the dreamer because she awakened with a sense of mission as a result of Christ's speaking to her, but she had only a very tentative perception of what the mission was.

Dream Story: A Vision of the Devil

The same woman reported this dream:

> I am at a coffee shop/sidewalk café. Across the street from me, I see the devil. He is sitting like a regal lion, four-legged, with a large, flowing mane and very smug facial expression. I ask him to leave me alone. He yawns with a roar and saunters away, saying, "I'm always around."

Dream Meaning

The context was the downtown setting, with no apparent change of context in the dream. The interaction with the Satan figure formed the bulk of the dream experiences. The perception of Satan's power, the woman's request, and the devil's threatening exit formed an experience base that was tied to her fear and the apparent autonomy of her adversary. Finally, the dream ended with the antagonist wandering off and the dreamer being left alone.

DREAM COACHING

There were two major influences from the dreamer's waking life that had an impact on this dream. The first was that the woman had experienced a near-fatal illness. She felt it was an expression of evil in her life. Second, she readily admitted that she had not pursued her spiritual life. She felt that the illnesses that afflicted her and her cousin were beyond human ability to integrate independently of the Divine. Consequently, she both wanted and rejected that connection in her waking life. This intellectual dissonance seemed to be the trigger event for both dreams.

To help her with this, I talked to her about how everyone must face mortality. The issue of our own mortality and that of those we love is too great for us to manage independently, without looking to our spiritual resources. Various spiritual traditions deal with this question differently, but all offer a helpful perspective on the inescapable fact of our mortality.

CHAPTER 31

Dreams That Tap into Universal Reality

*I dream in my dream the dreams of all the dreams of the
other dreamers and I become the other dreamers.*

—Walt Whitman

Some dreams come to you to help you see more clearly and cope more accurately with the world you live in by showing you life as it is. Dreams like this are particularly useful because they invite you to accept the full implications of living in the world.

These dreams are important because they let you think about the things that you routinely put out of your mind in order to function as a person. For example, driving is a relatively hazardous activity. Space travel, flying, and parachuting are all statistically safer, but you let yourself drive every day because you must.

Dreams that tap into the universal remind you about the truths you sometimes neglect in the interest of peace of mind.

Dream Story: Walking Backward

A 16-year-old boy reported dreaming:

> *I'm watching TV. They are talking about terrorism, the World Trade Center, and all manner of anxiety. When I get up to walk, I realize that I am only capable of walking backward and must turn my head and strain to see where I'm going. Then the scene changes, and it's like that movie, Liar, Liar. As I'm walking along with some family members, everything and everyone states the truth regardless of the consequences. It's funny, but kind of scary.*

Dream Meaning

In this dream, several realities of becoming a mature person in the world confronted the dreamer all at once. He realized that as he tried to anticipate his life in the world, his vision was limited. Only when he looked at the past could he see clearly what had happened. This is true for all of us, no matter how insightful we are.

The news doesn't tell us what's going to happen, it reports what has happened. There's no source of information about what's going to happen. All we can really do about the world is prepare for the worst, hope for the best, and accept something that falls approximately between the extremes most days. Looking back, even if only to a time moments ago, is all we really have available to us.

DREAM COACHING

I observed, "I think you're getting a little cynical about life."

"Well, all these adults have been trying to control the world, and they've just messed it and me up," he said.

The soul coaching from this dream was a real gift to this young man. Much of his energy went into reacting to people and events. After this dream, he realized that the world he was entering wasn't already cast in stone. He had the opportunity and privilege of building a future that was truly his own. In order to experience that potential, he would have to stop looking backward at what had happened and why, and begin to look forward at what could happen.

Another kind of universal dream gives the dreamer empathy with others going through the cycle of life in ways that we don't understand through experience but that we observe. For example, you may not know what it's like to feel yourself reaching old age or living in a war zone, but these are two realities that many people face.

Dream Story: Running from Bombs

A woman in her forties recounted the following dream:

> *I am vacationing with my parents. We enjoy a large and beautiful apartment. Large stones/bombs begin falling on people randomly, causing significant head wounds. We run for shelter in a gymnasium. The ceiling in the gym begins to show cracks, and I wonder what will happen next.*

DREAM COACHING

I asked her, "Experiencing a little prewar empathy?"

"I did wake up feeling a lot of empathy for the people in Iraq," she replied. The dream occurred about a month before the start of hostilities between the United States and the government of Saddam Hussein.

The dreamer realized very acutely that as a result of the war, the Iraqi people— even those who had nothing to do with the ruling regime—would be exposed to significant pain. She very much wished that there were a better, more humane option. However, given the reality of the impending war, she wanted to look at it realistically and not romantically.

A follow-up question got an interesting response. "Are you starting to perceive your parents' mortality more clearly, and are they talking to you about it?" No matter what your age, your parents form an archetypal "cover" for your life. As long as they are alive, regardless of their physical or mental condition, you still have that older generation to protect you from the full recognition of the frailty of life.

"I was having a conversation with my dad, and he mentioned feeling as though there's a bullet out there with his name on it," she said. "He's had several illnesses and deaths in his extended family this year."

The woman's dream showed not only the pain of others who experience loss but also the limitations of the "cover." When you're confronted with the mortality of your parents, you're exposed to the truth that you won't always have that "covering" available to you. Eventually, you will be the oldest branch on the family tree.

The interpretation is basically the same for both this woman's dream and that of the boy in the previous story: The dreams are showing the world more clearly to the dreamers. The soul is calling for them to accept and make inner changes based on seeing the world as it really is.

CHAPTER 32

Will You Dare to Dream?

Our dreams are a second life. I have never been able to penetrate
without a shudder those ivory or horned gates which separate
us from the invisible world.

—Gerard Nerval, French novelist

Dreaming of a big house, a great job, an attractive partner, or a fancy car—wishing for life to reward you—is easy. Many dreams fall into the category that Cinderella called "a wish that your heart makes." These dreams focus on changing the external circumstances of life with little or no examination of your soul. They are simply fun and recreational.

Dreaming that motivates the character in you to move from where you are right now to where you want to be in life is an entirely different, and more rewarding, proposition. The soul is speaking, challenging you to grow. The question is, Will you dare to dream?

This kind of dreaming focuses on changing your interior life to move you toward the well-being of your soul. Your dreams are trying to do that every night. The question is, Will you dare to listen?

Dreams That Bring Growth over Time

Vanessa, a single woman approaching 40, was not getting where she wanted to go. She hoped for more but constantly found herself settling for less or having demands inflicted upon her by others. Her soul was eager to point her toward the best and highest expression of her life.

Dream Story: A Wish for Reconnection

The first dream narrative she related involved a relationship with a man:

> *I am talking on the phone with my ex-boyfriend. I can hear that he is holding a baby, and he sounds incredibly happy.*

Dream Meaning

Like so many people, she was eager to hear a prophetic interpretation of her dream. There was an underlying tone of, "Please tell me this is going to happen."

She was recovering from a painful breakup of a nearly 10-year relationship. If she could justify pursuing reconciliation, she would. She said, "He has been my life for the last 10 years. If we can get back together, I will be happy to wait for him." The desire for a prophetic interpretation was very high.

We went to work on the phone, baby, and happiness experiences in the dream. The phone is a way to be both with and not with someone simultaneously. The baby was in his immediate presence, while the phone was the only connection to his former lover. The happiness he felt was because of his proximity to the baby, not to her. She intuitively hinted at that interpretation by reporting that he held "a baby" rather than "our baby." The baby was not "theirs."

Vanessa's dream was about his preference for being connected to his boyish self rather than having a genuine connection with her. The influence of his own "babyish" immaturity was more attractive to him than real connection with another person. The result was that he was happiest apart from her and living exclusively for himself.

In the relationship, she had been the responsible one; he was the troubled one who couldn't quite get it together. I braced myself for a reaction and asked what I already suspected was true, "Was your relationship pretty painful due to some indulgences of his?"

"He had issues with alcohol and cheated on me a couple of times," she admitted.

On the surface, his boyish charm was attractive and winsome to her. Many times in the relationship, however, she had found herself absorbing consequences or compensating for his immaturity. His tendencies toward womanizing and alcohol had plagued the relationship.

Vanessa and I spoke at length about men and relationships, how she had lost herself in nurturing his needs, and how her efforts to be "good enough" for him ultimately undermined his sense of connection with her. The more their relationship was about his needs, the happier he was. When Vanessa thought they were on the verge of true intimacy and marriage, he broke off the relationship.

Her soul's lesson in this was that she needed to stand up for herself more—and earlier—in relationships and not tolerate emotional abuse such as her ex-boyfriend inflicted on her. His happiness had come at her expense.

We spoke about how she needed to find support for herself in future relationships so that a man's immaturity wouldn't become so painful an experience for her. If she developed her inner resources so there was more "Vanessa" to relate with, she could have more peace as an unattached person and ultimately experience more emotional connection when relationships became available again.

Dream Story: Unearthing a Christ Figure

As Vanessa started working on this agenda, she had another dream:

I am cleaning out the closet in the house we shared [they actually shared this house in waking life]. *I come across a Christ statue in a dresser drawer in a closet. I handle it with a familiarity that means it must be mine, even though I don't remember "owning it" as such.*

Dream Meaning

As she grieved the relationship, Vanessa realized she had lost parts of her identity in pursuing her boyfriend. When she was younger, she had enjoyed faith convictions that brought order and structure to her life. However, the longer her relationship had continued, the more she had abandoned what she thought was right for what seemed the right way to stay connected with her boyfriend. This compromise ultimately worked against commitment, sabotaging her aspirations for her life, marriage, family, and so on.

DREAM COACHING

I asked, "Do you still have any faith in God? Perhaps more important, do you think God has any faith in you?" Although Vanessa had confessed to deeply held faith convictions, those convictions had been "under cover" during the relationship. She realized, very painfully, that by not seeking relationship in the context of her faith, she had sacrificed herself in her efforts to please another person.

When the relationship had been close and passionate, her lover was her "world." Now in the grieving process, she struggled to understand where in the world she belonged, or to whom. The soul hungers for connection with the transcendent, especially when human relationships disappoint us.

Her recurring question was, "How did I get so far off-course?" In fact, her soul was now helping her work on that question by comparing what had been with what would have been best. Her faith convictions had proffered a relationship structure that supported her goals and aspirations for commitment and relationship. Her actions had led somewhere else, to isolation and sadness.

Certainly, it is possible to experience broken relationships with your faith intact. However, when Vanessa realized how far afield she was from the life she wanted, she understood that perhaps she had become disconnected from an understanding of the Divine that could help ease the hurt she felt.

Because she felt unlovable to another person to whom she had given herself completely, she wondered if she was lovable to God. The soul was created for intimacy and connection. It seems unthinkable that the Divine would create us to be loved and then deem a person unlovable. We spoke for a long time about the Divine's capacity to love her in the midst of her hurt.

I also asked about her father. The dream hinted that perhaps her father had been emotionally unavailable to her and that she had repeated that experience by loving a man who was equally unavailable.

Her father, who had died several years earlier, was an immigrant. His effort and commitment to build their home had undermined his connection with the children, and he had not been there for her emotionally. She had wondered if she was ever really "good enough" for him.

The dream of the Christ figure was not a dream just about faith but also about earthly relationships as well. The rejection implied by her father's conduct toward her at times, the rejection of her lover, and the seeming rejection of the Divine appeared to be the same—a rejection that left her wondering who she belonged to, as well as who belonged to her.

The healing process could begin in earnest for Vanessa once she realized that she was lovable. The emotional unavailability of her father, recapitulated by her boyfriend, reflected on a hurt place in her soul. If she could forgive her father for his shortcomings, perhaps she could give herself permission to connect with men who were attainable.

Dream Story: Familial Reconciliation

Later, a third dream presented itself:

> *I am standing before my father. I bend down and kiss him on the fore-head* [not realizing or worrying that he is dead; he didn't "feel" that way to her]. *I turn and walk away from him, feeling strangely peaceful about the whole exchange.*

Dream Meaning

This dream signaled a revolution in Vanessa's inner life. Rather than trying to get love, connection, and affirmation from her father, she now offered it to him through forgiveness. Instead of feeling guilty that she wasn't "enough" for her father, she grieved for his inability to respond to who she was.

D R E A M   C O A C H I N G

This dream message pushed a series of buttons in Vanessa and increased her determination: No longer would she pursue men to get connection with them. Instead, she gave herself permission to experience connection as it came to her with value and emotional substance. This liberation was frightening at first, because it challenged Vanessa to be okay with herself rather than feeling okay only if an "unreachable" man validated her.

A series of dreams about her father ensued, often revolving around the last days of his life and conciliatory gestures toward him. Sometimes he initiated the reconciliation, and sometimes she did. Altogether, these dreams offered Vanessa the resources she needed to grow a healthy connection with her self, her dating, and her aspirations through her faith. In each dream, her soul provided deep inner direction so that she could be liberated from other people's all-consuming demands and draw upon the growth resources inherent in her soul.

It was a slow, organic process. For the first 40 years of her life, Vanessa had attempted to fill a particular void she felt in life, and the void had turned into a bottomless chasm of unreciprocated feelings of love. The dream wisdom from her soul began a process that was a daring act of deliverance from the life she was living: brokenhearted in romance, isolated from the Divine, and wounded by her earthly father's struggles. When she dared to dream, she chose the life she was really intended to live: free of her past codependence, healed from the hurts of her childhood, and connected to an authentic faith that gave her a sense of belonging in the world.

Leaving Behind the Pain as You Undertake a Life of Greater Joy

When you dare to listen to and learn from your dreams, they call you from the pain of living through the grief of loss and toward resolution. Your dream wisdom shows you what isn't working and why. Then it confronts you with inner resources you are missing. Whether you never had access to them or have lost them is irrelevant. To heal, you must acknowledge their absence and then reconnect in relationships that nurture healthy emotions.

In contrast, when you live life by instinct, it calls you away from true resolution and toward pain. As long as Vanessa denied her father's imperfection, she couldn't grieve those feelings and experiences. Moreover, as long as she internalized feelings of inadequacy rather than grieving them, she didn't have the emotional resources or ability to move forward. She also tried to deny feeling that a relationship without commitment was unacceptable.

By wholeheartedly embracing her dreams, Vanessa was working through this dynamic. Her instincts were to choose men who were somewhat inaccessible. When their boyish attractiveness turned into the inability to commit and connect, she wound up back at the place of pain that had been with her since childhood—the pain of not being connected with a man she genuinely wanted to please.

DREAMS IN THE BIBLE

In the Hebrew Scriptures and Christian New Testament, there are several prominent dreams and dream interpreters. For example, Jacob dreamed of a ladder ascending to the heavens, used by the angels to journey to Earth. Joseph, the son of Jacob and great-grandson of Abraham, used dreams to understand his role in the family, to extricate himself from being wrongly imprisoned, and to guide a nation through poverty and drought. Some 800 years later, Daniel believed that dreams revealed the course of world affairs, as the empires of the ancient Near East gave way to the rising influence of the West. If you use the word "vision" as a synonym for "dream," the list grows significantly.

In the New Testament, both Joseph, the father of Jesus, and the magi were guided by dreams or visions that protected the Holy Family. At the occasion of Jesus' trial, Pilate's wife complained to him that dreams about Jesus of Nazareth troubled her in her heart. As St. Paul was planning his journeys, he received dream wisdom to direct his endeavors. Part of the book of the Revelation of St. John seems to be derived from dream narratives as well.

Since a divine spark resides in the soul of each of us, when the Divine wishes to communicate with us, it commonly uses dreams to do so.

CHAPTER 33

Recovering from Broken Dreams

What happens to a dream deferred?
Does it dry up like a raisin in the sun;
Or fester like a sore and then run?
Does it stink like rotten meat;
Or crust and sugar over like a syrupy sweet?
Maybe it just sags like a heavy load.
Or does it explode?

—Langston Hughes

If you will dare to dream, there is one unavoidable issue of life. Some of your dreams or aspirations will be broken. Sometimes your personality will neglect the soul's call for well-being in favor of lesser appetites. Obviously, a dream is not a material thing that can be damaged or destroyed. Nevertheless, dreams do break, sometimes into a thousand pieces, and they can't be glued back together.

What is a "broken dream"? A dream emanates from who you are. When an expectation goes unmet or an aspiration is deferred, the part of you embodied by that hope breaks away from the rest of your life. Thus, a broken dream reflects a broken part of you.

To move along in her healing journey, Vanessa, whose story I told in the previous chapter, had to grieve a couple of broken dreams before she could pursue the life she truly wanted. She had to grieve the isolation she had felt from her father early in her life and the time invested in a relationship that failed.

The hurt of the broken dreams in her life, as in all lives, needed time to be comforted. The reason is that when you keep pursuing dreams without recovering from broken ones, there is no growth, just repetition.

In Vanessa's case, she needed to break the cycle of "I'm going to try to be 'good enough' for a man who doesn't express love back to me." From an early age, she had absorbed a message from her father that she was not completely lovable. When she dreamed of reconciliation with her dad, it was a gesture from her soul of where her personality needed healing. What a gift! She could forgive her dad his shortcomings as a parent rather than approaching life from a "one-down" position in which she was always subservient.

Coping with Pain and Grief from Loss and Separation

Suppose you always envisioned yourself becoming a parent. If you defer that goal due to physical or relationship difficulties that you perceive as insurmountable, that dream will be broken. Moreover, the grief of that loss may significantly affect your idea of yourself and your capacity to experience relationships with people who have children. To become spiritually whole and mature, you have to resolve that broken dream.

For many people, the goal of being a parent is part of their lives long before the reality is possible. When that aspiration isn't fulfilled, the pain and grief of alienation take hold. Whether the inability to reach the goal is due to health challenges, relationship dysfunction, or personal turmoil, there is nevertheless a profound sense of loss or separation from life as it was envisioned. How wonderful it would be if we could find a resolution for this conflict!

What happens when you continually have broken dreams? The result is death by degrees. Perhaps the cues and signals of dreams can, in themselves, guide you away from brokenness and toward the life you feel you are intended, created for, or meant to live.

Fixing Broken Dreams

Perhaps your dreams can show you the resources necessary for healing and restoring your self. Perhaps your image of the self you envision needs to be redirected. Not every pleasurable, powerful experience is "right," nor is every unpleasantness of life undesirable. Again, your own soul may know and be calling attention to the path you must pursue. The trick is learning to listen.

Sometimes you find that people and resources come into your life so you can experience a second chance (or even a third or fourth chance) at hope, love, and reconciliation.

One of the best ways to fix broken dreams is to be with a group of people who can help you see clearly how your dreams speak to your life. For this to work, you need a group that shares a similar framework for growth and allows the wisdom of dreams to speak gifts of truth.

In addition, you need a workable framework for growth. Farmers don't toss seeds into the air and hope for a crop. They deploy their resources carefully, according to a master plan. You need a plan that stands independent of your circumstances to guide you toward effective growth.

This is where a dream group can be instrumental in helping you move forward. A community of fellow travelers on the journey toward wholeness is an indispensable resource for a person committed to growth of any kind.

DREAM METAPHORS

Language is the only way we have to communicate thoughts. Often, we use word pictures to capture nuances and meaning. For example, the phrases "fouled up" and "messed up" clearly describe a situation that is chaotic or out of control.

Dreams may use the language of metaphor. A married man who dreamed he was at a picnic eating a hot dog suddenly remembered a scene from his childhood in which his father's infidelity was characterized by the words, "You think you're some kind of hot dog." In fact, the dreamer had given serious consideration to an extramarital affair.

When you reflect on the signs and symbols of your dreams to determine their meaning, view them as metaphors and word pictures that can help you elicit additional nuances to apply to daily living. While you may not always come up with the best or most applicable interpretation, sometimes you can work through a more difficult or obtuse symbol by seeing it as a metaphor.

Conclusion

Where is it now, the glory and the dream?

—William Wordsworth

Where did your soul lead you last night, and where does it want you to grow today? The wisdom of your dreams is uniquely qualified to answer those questions. The answers come in the form of a process, not a recipe.

In the dream stories presented in this book, you have read about people seeking to understand life in the real world by understanding their dreams. When we worked together on their dreams, I tried to point them to the inner resources that would enable them to function more effectively in the waking moments of life. The soul, the divine spark (or *imagio dei*), was speaking to guide the dreamers toward the lives they were meant to live. Their dreams were invitations to join the process of growth. Although the dreamers intuitively knew the voice was speaking, they did not yet understand what it meant.

In modern culture, we're inclined to choose a recipe over a process, but recipes don't yield something edible until the ingredients are cooked, subjected to energy over time. A simple recipe for dream interpretation will leave you feeling empty and unsatisfied because you haven't converted your dreams into something you can metabolize.

A dream "recipe book" alone cannot bring forth your dream wisdom, because no two people possess exactly the same body of ingredients. Your mind is a unique gift, and your soul is singular in the entire universe.

Dreams are an ingredient—an important ingredient—in the process of living. When you treat them as such and expose them to the energy of your waking life, you can integrate them into your experience and your conscious moment-to-moment living.

I hope you are now eager to train yourself to be an active listener to the voice of your soul. When you learn the desires of the soul to connect you with yourself, others, and the Divine, you are ready to listen. As you begin to focus on the process, your soul will yield some incredible fruit.

Let your dreams call you forward into healthy, proactive growth that strengthens your spirit and expands your life. It won't necessarily be easy, but it can be the most rewarding experience of your life. As you learn the process of growth, I hope you will come to love it.

One of the questions you may ask is, "How will I know if it's working?" As your soul is freed to perform reparative work in your life and personality, you'll observe the rewards of its presence. Like an acorn that grows into a mighty oak, you, too, will blossom and grow.

In the process of the soul, the evidence of growth is the fruit of spiritual maturity: love, joy, peace, patience, kindness, goodness, faithfulness, gentleness, and self-control. These are the necessary qualities for you to experience a life marked by the dimensions of soulful existence.

Until then, sweet dreams.

About the Author

David C. Lohff, author of *Dream Coaching, The Dream Directory,* and *Dreams Cyclopedia,* is on the faculty of George Washington University School of Medicine. He has served as a dream coach for the *Regis and Kathy Lee Show.*

He is an experienced, certified marriage counselor, having completed a two-year residency with Washington Pastoral Counseling Services. David also counsels individuals in his role as pastor of College Parkway Baptist Church in Arnold, MD. He was endorsed for military chaplain service by the Southern Baptist Convention in June 1997.

His mission is to help people strengthen their personal relationship to God.

David and his wife Kathy have been married for over a decade. They met while students at Southern Baptist Seminary in Louisville, KY. They are the parents of five children: triplets Sam, Emily, and Matthew; and two younger daughters, Katie and Lauren. They live in Severna Park, Maryland.